COUNTERING ADVERSARIAL PROPAGANDA: CHARTING AN EFFECTIVE COURSE IN THE CONTESTED INFORMATION ENVIRONMENT

HEARING

BEFORE THE

SUBCOMMITTEE ON EMERGING THREATS AND CAPABILITIES

OF THE

COMMITTEE ON ARMED SERVICES HOUSE OF REPRESENTATIVES

ONE HUNDRED FOURTEENTH CONGRESS

FIRST SESSION

HEARING HELD
OCTOBER 22, 2015

U.S. GOVERNMENT PUBLISHING OFFICE

97–493

WASHINGTON : 2016

SUBCOMMITTEE ON EMERGING THREATS AND CAPABILITIES

JOE WILSON, South Carolina, *Chairman*

JOHN KLINE, Minnesota
BILL SHUSTER, Pennsylvania
DUNCAN HUNTER, California
RICHARD B. NUGENT, Florida
RYAN K. ZINKE, Montana
TRENT FRANKS, Arizona, *Vice Chair*
DOUG LAMBORN, Colorado
MO BROOKS, Alabama
BRADLEY BYRNE, Alabama
ELISE M. STEFANIK, New York

JAMES R. LANGEVIN, Rhode Island
JIM COOPER, Tennessee
JOHN GARAMENDI, California
JOAQUIN CASTRO, Texas
MARC A. VEASEY, Texas
DONALD NORCROSS, New Jersey
BRAD ASHFORD, Nebraska
PETE AGUILAR, California

KEVIN GATES, *Professional Staff Member*
LINDSAY KAVANAUGH, *Professional Staff Member*
NEVADA SCHADLER, *Clerk*

CONTENTS

Page

STATEMENTS PRESENTED BY MEMBERS OF CONGRESS

WITNESSES

APPENDIX

COUNTERING ADVERSARIAL PROPAGANDA: CHARTING AN EFFECTIVE COURSE IN THE CONTESTED INFORMATION ENVIRONMENT

House of Representatives,
Committee on Armed Services,
Subcommittee on Emerging Threats and Capabilities,
Washington, DC, Thursday, October 22, 2015.

The subcommittee met, pursuant to call, at 2:08 p.m., in room 2212, Rayburn House Office Building, Hon. Joe Wilson (chairman of the subcommittee) presiding.

OPENING STATEMENT OF HON. JOE WILSON, A REPRESENTATIVE FROM SOUTH CAROLINA, CHAIRMAN, SUBCOMMITTEE ON EMERGING THREATS AND CAPABILITIES

Mr. WILSON. Ladies and gentlemen, I would like to call this meeting of the Emerging Threats and Capabilities Subcommittee of the House Armed Services Committee to order.

I am pleased to welcome everyone here for today's hearing on information operations and counter-propaganda capabilities. This hearing will focus on the challenges faced by the Department of Defense [DOD] and the Federal Government when dealing with the insidious propaganda and social media messaging coming from groups like Daesh, and sadly, from countries like Russia, China, and others. Not only do they recruit members, raise money, and sway the opinion of potential allies with this propaganda, but they sow doubt and dissension as a means of preventing or discouraging U.S. military action to protect American families.

Last month, our subcommittee held a closed roundtable discussion with outside industry and academic experts to explore this topic. That discussion helped our members better understand some core challenges and concerns, including what are our current capabilities for information operations and counter-propaganda, and how are they being integrated into larger strategies to deal with specific actors like Daesh, Russia, Iran, China, and others.

How can new techniques and concepts improve our ability to sense, detect, analyze, and respond to propaganda in the 21st century media environment? What policy changes impair our ability to realize the full potential of these new technologies and concepts? These questions and issues remain relevant in today's hearing.

Our panel of expert witnesses will proceed from that starting point and provide us with their thoughts from a governmental perspective on this important topic.

Our witnesses before us today are Mr.—the Honorable Michael Lumpkin, Assistant Secretary of Defense for Special Operations and Low-Intensity Conflict [SO/LIC]; the Honorable Matthew Armstrong, Broadcasting Board of Governors [BBG]; Major General Christopher K. Haas, Director of Special Force Management and Development, United States Special Operations Command, SOCOM, and also a very grateful dad of a Citadel cadet, which I respect very much; and Brigadier General Charles Moore, Deputy Director for Global Operations, Joint Staff.

I would like now to turn to my friend and ranking member, Jim Langevin from Rhode Island, for any comments he would like to make.

[The prepared statement of Mr. Wilson can be found in the Appendix on page 27.]

STATEMENT OF HON. JAMES R. LANGEVIN, A REPRESENTATIVE FROM RHODE ISLAND, RANKING MEMBER, SUBCOMMITTEE ON EMERGING THREATS AND CAPABILITIES

Mr. LANGEVIN. Thank you, Mr. Chairman. I want to thank our witnesses for being here, for your service to the country, and for all you are doing to keep us safe. The Department of Defense's ability to work in concert with other U.S. Government agencies and international entities to effectively counter propaganda is an issue that the members of this subcommittee have been concerned with for some time, and I am glad, Mr. Chairman, that again you are holding this hearing.

DOD has a long history of countering adversary propaganda and influence in order to further our national security objectives, and it has met with great success. However, unlike World War II or in the 1980s, today's state and non-state actors disseminate their messages far and wide instantaneously, crossing multiple combatant command areas of responsibility and reaching audiences all over the world, including U.S. citizens.

Unfortunately, time and distance are no longer on our side. This evolution of the information environment forces us to think about how to approach this issue. Should decisionmaking within the military chain of command be decentralized so efforts can be more effective in time and space? If so, how do we maintain oversight and synchronization of efforts?

Further, how do we take into account privacy, freedom of speech, and other issues as they pertain to U.S. persons and nonadversaries in an environment without boundaries? Essentially, how can we more effectively employ capabilities?

As the chairman mentioned, the subcommittee held a roundtable with independent witnesses on the issue several weeks ago, setting the stage for a deeper discussion of the aforementioned issues.

Today, I look forward to hearing from our witnesses as to how they are working to more effectively employ capabilities that we do have and developing even better capabilities and tactics, techniques, and procedures for the future.

With that, Mr. Chairman, I look forward to our witnesses' testimony, and I yield back.

Mr. WILSON. Thank you very much, Mr. Langevin. I would like to remind our witnesses that your written statements will be submitted for the record, so we ask that you summarize your comments to 5 minutes or less, and then after that, we will proceed with each member having 5 minutes to ask questions.

We have a person who is above reproach, Kevin Gates, as we maintain the 5-minute rule, and then this is a unique hearing, and so we will actually begin with questionings in reverse order of how the seating, and we will begin with Congresswoman Elise Stefanik when we begin questions.

So I would like to thank again all of you for being here today, and we begin with Mr. Armstrong.

STATEMENT OF HON. MATTHEW C. ARMSTRONG, BROADCASTING BOARD OF GOVERNORS

Mr. ARMSTRONG. Thank you, Mr. Chairman, members of the subcommittee, thank you for inviting me to speak to the unique role of the Broadcasting Board of Governors and the United States international media, and the role we play in advancing our national interest. I am pleased to join today's panel alongside my colleagues from the Department of Defense. I have a longer written statement for the record, and I will summarize that here.

This committee knows well that while today's increasingly interconnected world offers us a plethora of opportunity, it also provides challenges. From Crimea, to Syria, Northern Nigeria, and Southeast Asia, propaganda and censorship have used our increasingly networked world to not just seek to win the news cycle, but to shape the very choices of statecraft.

U.S. foreign policy cannot be effective if we do not appreciate how information shapes the actions of policymakers, institutions, and the public. The Broadcasting Board of Governors is a unique tool within this broader context. We are a 24/7 global media organization that oversees nonmilitary international media support supported by the U.S. Government, including the Voice of America [VOA], the Office of Cuba Broadcasting, BBG-funded grantees Radio Free Europe/Radio Liberty, Radio Free Asia, and Middle East Broadcast Network.

Our ultimate goal is to inform, engage, and connect people around the world in support of freedom and democracy through topnotch fact-based reporting. We broadcast in 61 languages and reach more than 215 million people each week. We are unique, however, in that we prioritize our contact to impact strategic audiences. Many of our reporters are not only from our target markets, but they also maintain extensive networks in them. They speak as locals. They know their audiences deeply.

We are called upon to operate in markets until private information dissemination is found to be adequate. Virtually, by definition, we target markets that are hard to reach, and at best, underserved by accessible, reliable, independent media. In short, there is no other agency or corporation like us that puts the audience first, that actively builds true independent media markets in order to one day not be needed.

By unleashing the power of professional journalism, we not only inform foreign publics, we allow individuals to aspire to freedom by offering them a platform to make decisions based on information that is verifiably true. When we cover the successes of free and open elections, as we have recently in Nigeria, for instance, we educate the audiences on how opposition parties can seek power through the ballot.

We serve as a key explainer of U.S. policy as well. VOA's charter mandates that our programs present the policies of the United States clearly and effectively, and also present responsible discussions and opinion on these policies. When we train the lens on our policy discussions, for example, by covering different views on recent negotiations with Iran, we allow the world to see democracy as a constantly evolving work in progress guided by the rule of law.

Even simply talking about how Americans go about paying a parking ticket can open the eyes of our audiences. Allow me to use some terms that are not usually associated with the BBG, but are familiar to the committee and to my colleagues at the table. The BBG is actively involved in foreign internal defense through empowering the people with the truth and giving them a voice through transparency and accountability. We work by, with, and through local populations by training and equipping local media and individuals to be better journalists. We actively work with some 3,000 affiliate news organizations around the world, including 400 radio stations in Indonesia alone.

We are a force multiplier for broader U.S. public diplomacy. We open markets and closed societies for fact-based journalism so the audience can see an alternative future. Our media provide a platform on which the Department of State, the Department of Defense, Agency for International Development, Agriculture, and others can build their own success.

As I had mentioned earlier, we face an increasingly networked world filled with challenges and opportunities. Let me mention five core—a couple of the core areas we are focused on. One, we are accelerating our shift toward engaged audience and digital platforms, video, mobile, social. Second, we are concentrating efforts in issue areas such as Russia, violent extremism, Iran, China. Third, we are focusing on impact overreach, putting the audience first.

We are focused—and last, we focus on challenging information and Internet freedom worldwide, which is an enduring and central role. Through our Internet Anti-Censorship Program and Open Technology Fund, we seek to support journalists, bloggers, civil society actors, and activists to use the Internet safely and without fear of interference. We underwrite apps and programs for computers and mobile devices that help encrypt communications and evade censorship. These efforts have been successful, and we look forward to expanding them.

As I close, let me say, journalism is a powerful force for change. By acting as the foreign domestic media, the BBG plays a critical role in the lives of the audiences by providing them with news and information in their local language that is relevant to their daily lives. Voice of America's first broadcast stated, "The news may be good or bad. We will tell you the truth." At BBG, we continue to operate with that in mind. Because truth builds trust and credibility, delivering credible news is the most effective counter to propaganda and ignorance, and provides the audience with information that will affect their daily lives and their daily decisionmaking.

And with that, I am happy to take questions. Thank you for your time and thank you for your attention.

[The prepared statement of Mr. Armstrong can be found in the Appendix on page 29.]

Mr. WILSON. And thank you, Mr. Armstrong. We now proceed to Secretary Lumpkin.

STATEMENT OF HON. MICHAEL D. LUMPKIN, ASSISTANT SECRETARY OF DEFENSE FOR SPECIAL OPERATIONS AND LOW-INTENSITY CONFLICT

Secretary LUMPKIN. Chairman Wilson, Ranking Member Langevin, and distinguished members of the committee, I appreciate this opportunity today to discuss the Department of Defense's role in direct support of the Department of State's efforts in the contested information environment.

I would like to thank the committee for your support in this critical field. I am pleased to be joined today by Brigadier General Moore and Major General Haas. It is good to have the—my counterparts here, and in proper reflection of the need of a whole-of-government response to this challenge, I am honored to sit next to Governor Matt Armstrong from the Broadcasting Board of Governors.

I am here to discuss an aspect of our information operations capabilities that has received special attention from this committee, and that is, our military information support operations force which requires—which provides a critical capability in support of tactical and operational needs of military requirements, as well as providing support to the overall strategic messages effort led by the State Department.

The scope of our current challenge in the informational space is unprecedented. In a Washington Post editorial on the threat posed by the Islamic State of Iraq and the Levant, ISIL, Under Secretary of State for Public Diplomacy and Public Affairs, Richard Stengel, estimated that only 1 percent of a potential audience of 1.6 billion people who could be targeted by ISIL's messaging will actually support ISIL's actions.

This 1 percent, while small at first blush, equates to approximately 16 million potential supporters of ISIL's actions around the globe. Even that startling number conceals a critical difference, which is the unfettered geographic and virtual dispersion of this new adversary.

Social media and other communications technologies has enabled the virtual, and in some cases, actual mobilization of dispersed and demographically varied audiences around the world. Non-state actors can reach across the globe with multiple, simultaneously targeted and tailored approaches to motivate or manipulate a spectrum of audiences.

They do this in numerous languages with messaging designed to specifically influence or motivate them according to their personal beliefs or perceptions, all conducted through smartphone, computer, and an Internet connection. In this environment, technology is not limited to one-way broadcast like television or radio, it allows interactive discussion any time in almost any location with virtually unlimited reach.

This hyper-connected world has many positive benefits, but the rise of ISIL and the ability for other state and non-state actors to conduct recruitment operations and spread propaganda almost certainly and with minimal cost highlights the dark side, one that requires the whole-of-government response.

In this challenging environment, I see two main implications for the Department of Defense. First, the Department does not lead the U.S. Government effort or possess the only capabilities in this space. All other civilian departments and agencies have their own roles and missions as part of the government's strategic communications efforts. This demands close interagency coordination and clear understanding of the appropriate roles and complementary nature for each piece of the U.S. Government's communication and engagement framework with global audiences.

The bottom line is that the Department's efforts alone cannot solve the challenge of this contested information environment and adversary propaganda, but we do have a critical role to play as a contributor of our unique military capabilities and a partner to the whole-of-government effort led by the State Department.

Second, the complexity of this environment demands that we use a thoughtful, strategic approach to achieve success against differing adversaries. Simply trying to master adversaries tweet for tweet, or Web site for Web site, is both fiscally irresponsible and operationally ineffective. Instead, we must rely on the skills of our talented workforce to develop thoughtful, well-constructed plans, partnerships with interagency and our international friends, and the use of a variety of means to disrupt the adversary's narrative.

We need to expose its contradictions and its falsehoods, and ultimately bring credible, persuasive, and truthful information to audiences who have often have significantly different perceptions and cultural norms than our own. We acknowledge and are appreciative of the intent of the language of section 1056 of the pending NDAA [National Defense Authorization Act].

Thank you for your support of the Department's efforts in this critical space, and I look forward to answering any questions you may have. Thank you.

[The prepared statement of Secretary Lumpkin can be found in the Appendix on page 40.]

Mr. WILSON. Thank you, Secretary Lumpkin. We now proceed to General Haas.

STATEMENT OF MG CHRISTOPHER K. HAAS, USA, DIRECTOR, FORCE MANAGEMENT AND DEVELOPMENT DIRECTORATE, U.S. SPECIAL OPERATIONS COMMAND

General HAAS. Mr. Chairman, distinguished members of the committee, thank you for the opportunity to discuss U.S. Special Operation Command's manning, training, and equipping of the military information support operations, MISO, force.

Preparing our MISO forces for current and future conflict is a critical role for USSOCOM [U.S. Special Operations Command]. The extensive propaganda efforts employed by both ISIL and Russia makes USSOCOM's role in manning, training, and equipping even more critical.

We have made significant improvements in all three areas over the last decade, but there is considerable work remaining, particularly improving our MISO force's capability to influence on the

World Wide Web. Now I would like to address SOCOM's role in manning, training, and equipping.

The overall end strength of the two Active Duty groups is approximately 1,050 officers and enlisted MISO soldiers. The active officer and NCO [non-commissioned officer] core is appropriately manned with the exception of sergeants at the E–5 level, which is below authorized levels. Our projections for recruitment and retention indicate we should have our Active Duty MISO groups fully manned by fiscal year 2019.

The complexity of the mission, and the expertise required to carry out MISO missions, has shaped an extended selection and training program for our MISO soldiers. They now attend a 2-week selection, and 42-week qualification course. This is different from other U.S. Government training, because it focuses on language, culture, and influence principles. This ensures our soldiers know how to design persuasive arguments, use the right symbols, and identify the best media. This training makes MISO a distinct asset within the Department of Defense.

As you well know, our adversaries use the Internet to recruit followers, gain financial support, and spread propaganda and misinformation. The current conflicts have identified our need to expand MISO training on the World Wide Web. Through the joint requirements process, multiple combatant commands have identified capability gaps in regards to MISO's use of the Web. SOCOM is now in the process of developing a comprehensive plan to expand MISO training into social media use, online advertising, Web design, and other areas.

Maintaining a current MISO equipment capability to meet our operational requirement is also an ongoing effort, but one USSOCOM is well-positioned to meet. We have a state-of-the-art media production center at Fort Bragg, North Carolina, with the capability to provide for print, audio, and video production. We are also constantly exploring and developing future MISO capabilities to ensure that we meet the emerging needs of the combatant commanders.

USSOCOM welcomes this committee's support regarding technology demonstrations to assess innovative and new technologies for MISO. The Web-based technologies we are exploring will be more flexible in nature and provide support to on-site commanders.

In closing, SOCOM is committed to meeting the challenges of training and equipping the force, while simultaneously addressing our current manning issues. I also want to thank you for your continued support of our SOF [special operations forces] personnel and their families. The tremendous demands we have placed on them requires a continued commitment to provide for their well-being and combat readiness. This concludes my opening remarks, and I welcome your questions.

[The prepared statement of General Haas can be found in the Appendix on page 54.]

Mr. WILSON. Thank you very much, General Haas. We will now proceed to General Moore.

STATEMENT OF BRIG GEN CHARLES L. MOORE, USAF, DEPUTY DIRECTOR FOR GLOBAL OPERATIONS, JOINT STAFF

General MOORE. Thank you, Mr. Chairman, Mr. Ranking Member, and distinguished members of the committee. I appreciate the opportunity to appear before you today to discuss the actions we and the Department of Defense are taking to counter the propaganda campaigns of our enemies.

In order to effectively achieve our military objectives and end states, information operations must be inherently integrated with all military plans and activities in order to influence and ultimately alter the behavior of our adversaries and their supporters. To accomplish that goal, there are several capabilities available to commanders, the most common being employment of our military information support operation forces, or MISO forces.

MISO personnel have the training and cultural understanding to assess enemy propaganda activities and propose unique solutions that directly support our ability to achieve our military objectives. MISO forces operating from a U.S. embassy and operational task force, or component headquarters, are employed to execute DOD missions that support named operations, geographic combatant commander, theater security cooperation efforts, and public diplomacy. How combatant commanders employ their MISO operation capabilities to counter adversarial propaganda is what I understand you want to focus on today.

MISO forces are currently deployed to 21 U.S. embassies working with country teams and interagency partners to challenge adversary IO [information operations] actions and support broader U.S. Government goals. To perform their missions, MISO forces use a variety of mediums, including cyber, print, TV, and radio, to disseminate information in a manner that will change perceptions, and subsequently, the behavior of the target audiences.

Unfortunately, as this is an unclassified hearing, the specific examples that I can discuss are limited, but I do want to provide you some brief examples of the efforts our MISO forces are currently undertaking around the world. In Central Command, MISO efforts are focused on challenging the actions of violent extremist organizations.

For example, in Iraq, MISO forces are conducting an advise-and-assist role, to help Iraqi forces learn to develop indigenous military information support operations and counter-propaganda activities. Central Command's online influence strategy is used to counter adversary narratives, shape conditions in the AOR [area of responsibility], and to message specific target audiences. These operations include using existing Web and social media platforms such as Facebook, Twitter, and YouTube, support military objectives by shaping perceptions while highlighting ISIL atrocities, coalition responses to ISIL activities, and coalition successes.

European Command's efforts include exposing Russian mistruths and their concerted efforts to mislead European audiences as to their true intentions. We are in the final stages of staffing European Reassurance MISO program, which will provide expanded authorities to conduct MISO training, and in some cases, messaging support to our partners in the region.

EUCOM [European Command] is also looking to expand their engagement with the Broadcasting Board of Governors to further improve their information dissemination capabilities.

Ultimately, regardless of the enemies that we face, the Department of Defense understands the criticality of countering an adversary supporter's confidence, conviction, will, decisionmaking, while shaping behavior supportive of our military objectives. We understand that these actions must be taken while not exceeding the authorities that we have been granted, while always operating within the boundaries the Department has been given, and with the close coordination of our interagency partners.

Finally, I also want to express my deep appreciation for the committee's unwavering support of our men and women in uniform, to thank you, again, for the opportunity to appear this afternoon, and I look forward to answer any questions that you might have. Thank you.

[The prepared statement of General Moore can be found in the Appendix on page 64.]

Mr. WILSON. Thank you very much, General Moore, and we now will proceed with the members' questions, and Kevin is going to make sure the clock is properly maintained. And so we will begin, of course, with Congresswoman Elise Stefanik.

Ms. STEFANIK. Thank you, Mr. Chairman. Thank you for your testimony today.

Secretary Lumpkin, my first question is for you. In October of 2014, the Department submitted a report to this committee on future military information operations capabilities as a result of section 1096 of the fiscal year 2014 NDAA. Can you give this committee an update on what progress has been made in implementing the findings and recommendations of that report?

Secretary LUMPKIN. Yes, ma'am. As mentioned in 2014, we answered that report, and we continue to develop and do this holistic review of how we do business, from everything from the authorities that we have in place, to the pieces of how we man, train, and equip, and to actually how we operate—operationalize our MISO efforts.

So this is part of our ongoing process, as we are always looking and reevaluating in dialogue with our interagency partners and with this committee and others to make sure we have the right oversight and we have the right capabilities in place.

So I think we are making good strides. Again, it is a continual challenge to work through, but I think we are doing the right things as we provide oversight and evaluate our capabilities.

Ms. STEFANIK. I wanted to follow up on the point you made about the authorities.

Secretary LUMPKIN. Uh-huh.

Ms. STEFANIK. Since we are operating in a very complex IO environment. At a previous hearing, we heard from the witnesses about the lack of clarity of the rules of engagement and of those authorities. Can you talk about some specific improvements that we should be making in order to clarify that?

Secretary LUMPKIN. I firmly believe that title 10 under U.S. Code gives DOD the authorities it needs to do the information operations that we are required to do to support our current mission, and the way—so I am very comfortable with our authorities in this space. We continue to work with our interagency partners to make sure that we are supporting them in the fullest and most robust way possible. And I—again, I do believe we have the authorities in place to do what we need to do.

Ms. STEFANIK. Thank you. My next question is for General Haas. Based on the current projections to reduce Army personnel by about 40,000 people, could you describe what effect these reductions could potentially have on the military information support operations community?

General HAAS. I would respond to that question this way, Congresswoman, is that the command is very concerned about the reduction in the overall size of the United States Army, from which we draw our pool of candidates for our MISO forces. It would be difficult for me to fully quantify that because the Army is currently in that process.

But as my commander has expressed in other forums, he is concerned about that drawdown, because that does reduce the pool of available candidates and qualified soldiers that would want to— that we could recruit, select, and train for our MISO force, and so we continually look and try to analyze, you know, exactly what that impact will be over time.

As I stated in my opening remarks, we are trying to mitigate some of these concerns through more active recruiting, directed specifically at the E–5 level, to fill our current shortages, and we are looking at other management tools in order to ensure that we retain our best qualified MISO soldiers in order to offset the potential impact of a smaller Army on our community.

Ms. STEFANIK. Thank you very much, and I yield back.

Mr. WILSON. Thank you very much. And we now proceed to Congressman Ashford of Nebraska.

Mr. ASHFORD. Thank you, Mr. Chairman. I have a couple of questions. One general one, and that is, in this area of recruiting individuals who can engage in this activity, General, how do you see, going forward with the authorities you have and some of the work that has been done in the NDAA, how do you see the private sector's expertise being tapped to raise the level of activity in this area? What is your vision of that?

General HAAS. Thank you for the question, Congressman. So SOCOM is exploring and is working on new relationships, not only with the private sector but with academia in general, trying to certainly garner the—and understand the skill sets that they can help in provide to—certainly to our community.

So that is an ongoing effort, and we are also partnering, as best we can, I think, with the interagency and we are looking for areas in which to improve that, so that we not only have a whole-of-government approach, but we have maybe a whole-of-society approach towards improving the quality of our MISO skills, knowledge, and abilities.

Mr. ASHFORD. And you believe you have adequate legislative authority to undertake those partnerships, I assume. Is that——

General HAAS. I would describe it this way: We have— USSOCOM has the adequate authorities to do our current man, train, and equip mission.

Mr. ASHFORD. Okay. So we can—having—well, let me give you an example. And maybe I misinterpreted what Admiral Rogers said, but I think I understood what he was saying in a committee hearing we had, that—so, for example, the—on the military side, we could reach out to the private sector, bring in expertise from the private sector to fill out the—some of these responsibilities on an interim basis or a short-term basis. Is that something—assuming that the standards are adequately adhered to, is that something that you all think could happen?

General HAAS. We obviously understand that the pace at which technology advances, we will probably have to reach out to the private sector in terms of contractors to bring that expertise into the force until we can appropriately train our soldiers, our men and women inside the MISO community to fully understand—operate and understand that new technology. And we are always working that balance between, you know, what is out there in the private sector and what we can then incorporate, gain into our community.

Mr. ASHFORD. Right. I think—let me ask General Moore. Could I ask you a question specifically about language competency? Hopefully I am asking—I think you talked about that a little bit, but when we were in Iraq with the chairman, there was discussion about, you know, the language, knowing the language—not only knowing the language, but knowing the nuances of the language, the different—and hopefully I am asking the right, Mr. Secretary, the right person here. Anybody can answer it. But are we—are we—that sort of sophisticated nuanced language training, is that—do we have the adequate—do we have adequate resources? You mentioned that is a challenge. There is maybe——

General HAAS. Yes, sir, that is more in my lane.

Mr. ASHFORD. Okay.

General HAAS. We spend a significant amount of our time in the qualification course for our MISO soldiers focused on language and culture, so the—each one of the MISO soldiers is required to graduate with a—what we call a one-one capability in a targeted language. And so that allows them to speak conversationally and read the language.

We are focused right now on a number of different languages, but we have adequate resources within the community to adjust that language, and then continually provide sustainment training. But as you know, mastering a language is sometimes a gift, and we look to target our soldiers with that gift in languages to——

Mr. ASHFORD. And do you recruit—sorry.

General HAAS [continuing]. So beyond one-one.

Mr. ASHFORD. Sorry. Do you recruit to that as well?

General HAAS. Obviously, in order to attend our assessment selection courses, those soldiers have to have an aptitude high enough score on their language test to enter our courses, so we do test to that.

Mr. ASHFORD. Thank you for your—for all your work. Thanks. Thanks, Mr. Chairman. I yield back.

Mr. WILSON. Thank you, Mr. Ashford. We now proceed to Congressman Trent Franks of Arizona.

Mr. FRANKS. Well, thank you, Mr. Chairman, and thank all of you. I always want to acknowledge the folks that wear the uniform and put themselves at risk for the rest of us in terms of even just putting your whole life to the cause of freedom, and I am grateful to you.

Essentially, I guess we are discussing the Department's capability today of, to use a quote here, "conducting operations to inform, influence, and shape adversarial behavior in the information environment." That sounds pretty important to me, given the ideological nature of some of the enemy that we face.

So I guess my first question is, what do you think represents the best bang for our buck, or the best strategic niche that we can pursue in order to actually change the behavior of our adversaries? And let's see, Secretary Lumpkin, I will go ahead and begin with you, and if anybody else would like to take the question, that would be great.

Secretary LUMPKIN. Yes. Thank you for the question. I think there is two principal aspects for us, is that one is that as part of DOD's larger strategy, it is all operations, large or small, have an information operation component that supports that particular operation. So it is codified and actually integrated in all operations. So I think that, first of all, that is kind of the chapeau that—so everything we do.

The other piece is that our relationships with the interagency where we look to how we can support our partners who have—and bring our unique military capabilities, whether it is print or it is working some other piece in order to help them in their effort.

So once our—our principal role here outside of doing information operations on operations, per se, that are uniquely military, is how we support our partners, so I think that is key and I think that is a huge value we bring as a Department.

Mr. FRANKS. Well, I have seen a lot of research that shows that one of the challenges that we have with this ideological enemy is that when we try to measure their commitment to their cause, that we sort of have to break it down typically to whether it is a sacred value to them or not. In other words, is this something that they are joining the group just for sort of the adventure, or if this is something that is deeply held conviction that goes to the religious core of who they are.

And it just—I am just wondering if these are really some of the leadership here is acting on sacred core values, and it doesn't seem like anything we can say to them is going to have a lot of impact, but it—perhaps our efforts would be redirected at those less committed so that we sort of—sort of impact the support base of the true believers, as it were.

Secretary LUMPKIN. All good points. It is very interesting. A study was recently done from a Lebanese-based company called Quantum, and it put ISIL, in particular, people into nine different bins of people who would join this organization, so it allows for better targeting. Just a quick list of them that I found were interesting.

The first one was the status seeker, somebody looking for status; the second one was an identity seeker, somebody looking for an identity; revenge, revenge seeker; redemption seeker; responsibility seeker; the thrill seeker; somebody who is looking for ideology, somebody who is looking for justice; and then a death seeker are the nine different bins.

So as things are developed, just as our enemies target specific audiences, the—we have to, as a U.S. Government writ large, have to have unique messages directed towards each of these nine different bins. I thought this was very informative and very helpful in helping me understand the problem awhile back.

Mr. FRANKS. Well, actually, you know, that is the point I was really trying to get to, as you probably imagine, and it sounds like that last guy is going to be a little bit recalcitrant. The death seeker doesn't sound to me like someone who is going to be open to a lot of, "well, you just had a bad childhood" approaches.

So I guess then my final question to you is, with apologies for this sequester and what it has done to pretty much the entire military apparatus of this country, do you feel like—and General Haas, this goes to your testimony, do you feel like the Department has the appropriate resources—you sort of touched on it already, but the appropriate resources and programming personnel to successfully execute this current counter-ISIL strategy? Do you think—and if you don't have something that you need, what could we do to make your life easier and more effective against these enemies of freedom?

Secretary LUMPKIN. If I may actually take that question. What I don't have is budget certainty. Where I am, I am trying to come up with a multiyear strategy, because this doesn't happen overnight. In order to influence somebody to change their mindset, their viewpoints, there is a continual engagement, so I am trying to do this in a multiyear plan on 1-year money.

Mr. FRANKS. Yeah.

Secretary LUMPKIN. So it is hard for us to make sound and longterm investments in our programming, in our planning to execute information operations without that budget certainty.

Mr. FRANKS. Yeah.

Secretary LUMPKIN. And Matt, do you have——

Mr. ARMSTRONG. Thank you. It is a similar situation. We are not sure what is happening.

Mr. FRANKS. Yeah.

Mr. ARMSTRONG. Is it possible to take a moment and answer your question as relates to——

Mr. FRANKS. Well, I guess, of course, as far as not knowing what is going to happen, given the potential veto, join the club, you know, we don't know, any of us know what is happening. Go ahead, sir. I want to be sensitive to my time here. My time is expired. If the chairman wants to extend the time for you to answer, that is great.

Mr. ARMSTRONG. Thank you. So you asked about the audience or the folks and the different ideological viewpoints and the realities. This is where I emphasize the particular nature of our toolkit, what we bring to the table.

The adversaries, and there are a whole bunch of different adversaries we face unfortunately right now, and they tend to rely on the say-do gap, they tend to rely on propaganda and a mistelling of history and a mistelling of the present, and they rely on the audience not knowing what the reality is, and they squash the freedom of speech and the freedom to listen, and that is where we are able to intervene and tell them what is actually going on, what is the truth.

And then an important element, whether it is an IO, public diplomacy, what we do is the trusted communicator, and we empower the people on the ground that are familiar, whether it is an affiliate radio station, or it is an individual that is familiar with the particular potential extremist to communicate and actually have the truth so that this individual is being impacted from all angles with the reality, what is actually happening, so that is another element where we are coming in.

Mr. FRANKS. Well, thank you, Mr. Chairman, for your indulgence here, and I think this gentleman could probably seek a career in political consulting at some point for campaigns afterwards. If you can change these guys' mind and help people see the truth, you have got a real future, brother.

Mr. WILSON. And thank you so much, Congressman Franks. We now proceed to Congressman Marc Veasey of Texas.

Mr. VEASEY. Thank you, Mr. Chairman. I wanted to ask specifically about some of the propaganda activities that we are seeing out there in different regions of the world, Russia, ISIL, and Iran, China. With there being such—with social media itself being such a challenge to counter, you know, rumors and innuendo and myths and what have you, how much can we reasonably expect to be able to challenge some of the things out there that we see from Russia or ISIL, or any of these actors that are using social media to really keep things stirred up?

General HAAS. I know from a SOCOM prospective, what we are looking at is how do we become more—much more proactive, and as I stated in my opening comments, we are undergoing an entire review based on combatant commanders requests that we take— that we take a closer look at what is happening on the Internet and social media sites, and then how do we help to influence that particular targeted audience via that media? And we've recognize that we are not on there constantly, and do we have the technology to be able to immediately respond and be a more—have a more persistent presence so that we can understand and then provide more comprehensive recommendations to our senior leaders and decisionmakers regarding the messages and other ways to counter this propaganda.

And so that comprehensive review, and that look at technology to enable us to do it is ongoing right now, and we are hopeful that by the first quarter, fiscal year 2017, we will have a better picture of how we are actually going to get after that problem set of being able to be more proactive and be involved in the discourse, you know, continuously, rather than basically shooting behind the target, or being in a tweet-for-tweet as the Assistant Secretary said, which we see only validates the message that they are sending out.

Mr. ARMSTRONG. If I may add, yes, we have to be proactive. One of the other challenges, and I think the general was getting to this, is we actually have to pay attention to the impact rather. The existence of the propaganda itself doesn't mean that there is impact. We have to look at what are they striving for and how do we counter that? How do we respond to that?

So often, the best counter is an indirect response. So we look at, for example, Iran, and much of the propaganda coming from Iran is trying to destabilize Iraq and Syria and wreak chaos, so if we are in there and talking about it or engaging on the subject matter of what we are actually doing, what is the reality on the ground there? That is helpful.

With Russia, much of the propaganda that surfaces is aimed at destabilizing the West, undermining the trust and credibility of journalism, of government, of NATO [North Atlantic Treaty Organization], of EU [European Union], and all those things, and so we can have a conversation along this other pathway, and we don't match propaganda. Certainly we don't go tweet-for-tweet, but we go to the overarching issues where they are having an impact.

And with Daesh, same thing, as I mentioned before, there is a say-do gap, and we start to hit them, hit the audience on what is the gap, what are they saying, but what is the reality? And this will help impact and reach the audience. And again, we empower that audience so that they start to recognize the propaganda for what it is. It is not effective to tell somebody that is propaganda. You have to get them to internalize, and then, again, have them be the communicator and share that experience.

Mr. VEASEY. In the state of affairs today, with everything going on with Russia, with ISIL, with Iran trying to keep things stirred up in the region, where should we be focusing most of our efforts as far as it pertains to counter-propaganda and counter-social media tactics?

Mr. ARMSTRONG. Well, sir, it is—that is a difficult question because each one of these is a unique threat, and it is a different environment.

Mr. VEASEY. Who do you think is the most effective out of those players in using the social media to cause discord?

Mr. ARMSTRONG. I suspect we would have different answers from different folks and the different marketplaces. I think each one of these are sowing a very critical threat. As I said, the Russian propaganda aimed at the non-Russian audiences aimed at undermining NATO, EU, government, media, and that is a very scary destabilizing influence if it is actually having the impact and it is a seeping impact onto the audience.

With Daesh, we see the impact of that, and there are questions on the resourcefulness of that, but honestly, I am not sure that— I think that is a above my pay grade, on where we should be focused. They are each unique threats, and it is based on our foreign policy and where we want to go.

Mr. VEASEY. Thank you, Mr. Chairman.

Mr. WILSON. Thank you, Mr. Veasey, and I will start my 5 minutes, and Kevin is pretty brutal about reminding me of this, which is good, and then we will proceed to Mr. Langevin. But as we begin, I want to indeed thank Mr. Armstrong, the Broadcasting Board of Governors. For you to have 61 languages, it is very impressive, too, for Voice of America to have persons who are actually proficient in the language, possibly even from—in their home community. That just comes across so positive and real world. I want to thank you for that.

And then General Moore, I was grateful to hear that at embassies, there are personnel, in a positive way, monitoring. I minored in journalism. I love print media. When I visit countries around the world, I enjoy picking up local newspapers and seeing what is available. I was in Islamabad, Pakistan, a couple of years ago and it was just a very positive newspaper that I read. It had dispatches from Reuters and from Associated Press. It had advertising giving an indication of a vibrant consumer society and competition.

But then I got to the op ed page, and there was a hate-filled column, and it was ridiculous. It was insane. And it was specifically about how the American military spends all of its time targeting mosques, hospitals, schools to achieve the maximum number of civilian mass murder, and I thought this is so insulting.

I mean, to the intelligence, in my reading it, who wrote it, and I looked: Fidel Castro. So it was somewhat discredited when I found out who the author was, but like entirely. But we have just got to be vigilant because somebody might believe the total and utter propaganda that I saw.

With that in mind, Secretary Lumpkin, how closely are the activities of our information operations capabilities and people linked with the cyber operation capabilities and personnel?

Secretary LUMPKIN. I am going to defer to General Moore on that question.

Mr. WILSON. That is fine. Thank you.

General MOORE. Yes, sir. Thank you for the question. They are extremely closely linked, as has been indicated several times so far in the discussions that we have been having. Organizations like ISIL are very, very dependent upon using cyber capabilities or the Internet, social media, through everything from command and control, disperse their propaganda, foreign fighter flow, and communications with regards to that, funding efforts, et cetera. So they are inherently linked.

And as you are aware, Mr. Chairman, I know cyber is just one of the many information-related capabilities that is part of a broader information operation paradigm or structure, and so all those things occur simultaneously.

Mr. WILSON. Well, we appreciate the effort very, very much. And General Haas, is there an overarching DOD, or Federal Government strategy to counter information operations and propaganda? How effective has it been? Or if not, what lack of strategy hindering our ability to take meaningful actions in the information environment?

General HAAS. Thank you for the question, Mr. Chairman. I am going to defer to the Assistant Secretary.

Mr. WILSON. Hey, this is great. I want the right person to answer the question.

Secretary LUMPKIN. No, no, thank you, Mr. Chairman. I appreciate the question. Again, the State Department is the lead for the whole of government—U.S. Government response in working in the information space. On the counterterrorism part, they have the CSCC [Center for Strategic Counterterrorism Communications], which is—manages that, and the rest is done through the bureaus at State. It is how they manage their regional messages, and we provide direct support again. And the CSCC, for example, there is

20-some-odd people who were working that particular mission set, and we are providing about 25 percent of them detailed over to the Department of State to assist them in that mission.

So we are very closely linked within the interagency with our partners as we continue to work this, this challenging environment. And again, going back to the DOD's strategy, not only is the inter-agency piece, but it is what I mentioned earlier is that piece where every one of our operations has an information operation component to it.

Mr. WILSON. Well, thank you very much, and Secretary, I appreciate you pointing out that the ISIL target may be only 1 percent, but that is 16 million people, and sadly, in my home State, we had a shooting at Ebenezer AME [African Methodist Episcopal] Church. It was somewhat of a backhanded compliment to the people of my State that the murderer identified he could not find people locally who agreed with him. But what motivated him was going on the Internet and finding people. And so what I had hoped would be liberating of Internet can actually produce an extraordinary danger to American citizens. And I now proceed to Mr. Langevin.

Mr. LANGEVIN. Thank you, Mr. Chairman. I, too, want to, again, thank our witnesses for your testimony.

So if I could, Secretary, maybe we can do a little deeper dive on this the whole-of-government approach, how information is managed, and can you talk more specifically? You say from the strategic to the down to the tactical, how we are managing the information, and the way in which the State Department has input into this as well as the IC [Intelligence Community] in terms of messaging, and again, how the information flows and how it is managed?

Secretary LUMPKIN. No, I appreciate the question, sir. Again, the State Department has the lead, so they set the conditions internationally, you know, as far as the messaging piece. We, at DOD, you know, we execute in support, you know, tactical- or operational-level military operations. We do that as we continue to work with the State Department in the larger message sets.

Now, the Intelligence Community, what they are doing is they are continually watching our adversaries' actions, and to see what they are doing and which feeds back into the process of we know what they are doing and how they are responding.

You know, the two principal challenges we have in this space within the Department is that, one, the speed of technology and what our adversaries are able do with it, so we are always adjusting and shifting; and there is also the assessment piece that we do all the time, because we have to assess if our actions are actually working.

And one of challenges we have that is kind of unique to this space is that when we—when something doesn't happen, something bad doesn't happen, that is frequently when we know we are successful. So we are trying to validate something that didn't happen. So it is a challenge. But as we work in the overall structure within the whole-of-government approach, that is always feeding back in as far as the whole process as we work with the IC, the State, and then DOD's component in there.

Mr. LANGEVIN. Is State properly resourced? And again, will they have some of the lead on this? But the capabilities are in the hands of DOD. Are they properly resourced to help to manage the information flow?

Secretary LUMPKIN. I think it is outside of my lane to talk about State Department resourcing. That said, the fact that we have, you know, 25 percent of the CSCC detailed to fill critical positions over there tells me they don't have the manpower to put against the mission like they would. That is my guess, but I would defer to State for a more satisfying answer.

Mr. LANGEVIN. That insight is helpful. I appreciate the answer. So Secretary, ISIL is waging, obviously, an information operations campaign using social media that has proven effective in recruiting new fighters, obtaining financing, and generally strengthening their political and strategic goals while undermining U.S. and other regional partners' objectives.

ISIL also uses open sources for command and control, and their broad use of social media has reinvigorated a discussion, obviously, of DOD's role and effectiveness in the information operations environment.

So little more—drilling down a little bit more on this topic, are Department of Defense's policies and directives keeping pace with the ever-evolving information environment? And what reviews and discussions are taking place within Department of Defense in whole of government to increase effectiveness of military operations to counter propaganda, and are new tactics, techniques, and procedures being developed?

Secretary LUMPKIN. We are doing continual self-evaluation, not just within the Department of Defense, but the interagency writ large. As a matter of fact, I sat in a meeting yesterday with Secretary Carter and Secretary Kerry, and this was one of the topics that we discussed is that how we continue to work better to counter and show the true nature of ISIL, and to make sure we are leveraging every asset authority that we have collectively between our two organizations to continue to show the world what ISIL really is.

So it is a continual process, and we look forward to our continued work with the committee here. If we do identify new needs or authorities, we will come to you asking for those.

Mr. LANGEVIN. Again, since my time is running out, I will wait to if we go to a second round of questions. But to Mr. Franks' question, the topic that he raised, and Mr. Armstrong, you talked about these trusted partners and seeking them out and making sure that the message is communicated; and Secretary, your point of exposing ISIL for what they are, finding, identifying those credible voices, particularly, for example, President al-Sisi and the speech that he gave to the religious community and the admonition that he gave, those are the types of things that help to convey the message of a counterbalance to what the message an organization like ISIL is trying to convey. With that, I will yield back since my time has expired.

Mr. WILSON. Thank you, Ranking Member Langevin. We now proceed to Congresswoman Stefanik.

Ms. STEFANIK. My question is for Mr. Armstrong. We have talked a lot today about the importance of countering propaganda with a credible voice. And you mentioned that in your testimony. But during a CODEL [congressional delegation] I was on earlier this year, in Jordan specifically, much of the leadership discussed the importance of the fact that this is a long-term, generational struggle. And again, instead of talking about our strategies for being reactive, what do we need to be doing to make sure that our IO capabilities are more proactive? I know that is a broad question, but I think it is an important one looking 5, 10, and a generation down the line.

Mr. ARMSTRONG. Thank you for the question. Because of the nature of my agency, I am going to restate the question slightly because we don't do information operations, but the information environment. It is important that the value of information, the value of the conversation, the value of journalism, the freedom to speak and the freedom to listen, and that empowerment to the audience, is maintained over the years. This agency is Voice of America, it started in the 1940s, 1942. And it has always had a fundamental purpose of empowering people through the access to news and information. And that was a fundamental counter to propaganda was access to the truth.

So I think the one answer is acknowledging that information matters. We forget that. It seems to come and go in waves.

Two, appreciate that in the United States, we have a fundamental appreciation of the press. And there is a reason why, because it is fundamental to a democratic process and whatever flavor of democracy that is. They are very important, they're a voice for the people.

Three, that the people actually matter and that they need a voice, not just the, quote, "formal journalist." And then I would add another is that our interagency partners can use us more, that they can be available to us to get on because of our access to the audience, they can come on and they can speak to a vast audience much greater than simply standing at a podium and hoping that a Western media will convey that story to a foreign domestic audience that is a target audience or that that local media, which often does not have a global reach and does not understand the context of the statement of say Secretary Kerry or the President or whoever it is going to be, and that they utilize us more because we can help unpack that story.

Ms. STEFANIK. General Haas, did you want to comment on that question?

General HAAS. Well, SOCOM specifically is working on not only the interagency aspect of this problem set, as the Secretary said, but we are also very focused on building reliable partnerships, which we see as critical to really informing us about this generational issue. And so we spend a lot of time at SOCOM and within our tactical forces building those important, reliable international partnerships that we will need to better inform us for the future.

Ms. STEFANIK. Thank you very much for those thoughtful answers. I yield back, Mr. Chairman.

Mr. WILSON. Thank you, Ms. Stefanik. I think an unheralded positive story has been the military information support operations. And I think it would be very helpful for General Haas, General Moore, possibly Secretary Lumpkin, if you all could explain how these are developed and what has been the experience for the last 14 years?

General MOORE. As far as the training and equipping, et cetera, that I know General Haas can get into the specifics for you there. But I will tell you that they have been absolutely critical, especially as I mentioned in some of the opening statements, in our embassies to help advance the capabilities of a lot of the governments and a lot of the military organizations that we have been helping in terms of building their partnership capacities, so that they can deal with these problems on their own, which, of course, I know you understand, ties right into really what our goals are in places like Iraq right now, which is to let them work these issues from the inside out.

So I think that they have been invaluable, and we will continue to use them whenever they are requested by the chiefs of mission, and supported by the relevant combatant commanders. General Haas.

General HAAS. The successes, as well as the lessons learned, have helped us inform SOCOM in how do we adjust our assessment selection process as well as our qualification process for our MISO soldiers? So every 2 years, we do a detailed review based not only on the successes that we are seeing in the AFRICOM [U.S. Africa Command] AOR with hunting Joseph Kony, to what we are experiencing in the Pacific AOR or the Central Command AOR to help us refine the actual classes of instruction, and the skills and attributes that we want to build into our MISO force.

So they have been very informative over the last decade, and they will continue to inform us in the future. So we are fielding a MISO force that meets the requirements of the specific combatant commanders. And if we have to, for example, adjust a language requirement based on an emerging requirement, then we have the capability to do that, and I think the flexibility within our system to adjust to meet that emerging requirement.

Mr. WILSON. And as I conclude, I want to thank you all. And something that was meaningful to me, by getting proper information out, it promotes a level of stability and certainly robs people who have ill intent to their local community and us. And I think in coordination with the United States Agency for International Development. I wish more people knew about that too. What was so inspiring to me on my 11 visits—12 to Afghanistan, to see the number of signs that were by road signs next to buildings of the clasped hands, U.S. flag, the flag of the Islamic Republic of Afghanistan.

And a point that always impressed me, many of these signs were rusty, they had been there a long time. And if people found that resentful of these schools being built, the hospitals being built, the bridges being built, they could take the signs down. And so much good. And I always quote Congresswoman Sheila Jackson Lee, and that is on my first visit to Afghanistan, that good news has no feet and bad news has wings. So good luck. And to the Board of Governors, please get all this corrected. I now go to Congressman Langevin.

Mr. LANGEVIN. Thank you, Mr. Chairman. Just one final question, I would go to General Haas. General, can you please describe, to the extent that you can in an unclassified forum, current information related to capabilities to counter propaganda and social media? Which are most effective in your opinion and why? And what challenges do forces face in employment of these capabilities? And how are these challenges being addressed? And what capabilities are being developed in the future—for the future, I should say?

General HAAS. Thank you for the question, sir. If I could break that down and answer it. Your first part was——

Mr. LANGEVIN. Which of the capabilities, to the extent that you can talk about it in an open forum, which are most effective and why?

General HAAS. Thank you. So as I said in my opening comment, I think the most important capabilities that we bring is our language and cultural understanding, as well as the training that we provide to our MISO soldiers on how to conduct influence ops, particularly in the 21 deployed military information support teams that General Moore talked about. That is one of the distinct capabilities that we help bring to the country team and the interagency, is this cultural understanding and awareness, as well as this language capability.

Now, as I stated, what we are looking to the future is addressing the Internet-based operations of the future. And we, in a different forum, we would be more than happy to discuss what we are determining in that current assessment of our capability gaps and where we see an opportunity to fill or close those gaps in our current capabilities.

Mr. LANGEVIN. Okay. Thanks, General. And I guess, you know, related to this, the other part of my question was what challenges do forces face in employment of these capabilities? And how are the challenges being addressed?

General HAAS. Well, I believe there is multiple challenges, depending upon which region of the world we are deployed. I think we have a great relationship with our interagency partners in this area. And I think our combatant commanders, without speaking for them, based on what they have identified, is that we are probably not capable or doing enough on the Internet or the Web. And that is what they have specifically asked us to address, those challenges. As to the other challenges, I would have to defer that to my Joint Staff partner or those specific combatant commands that are employing our MISO forces out there today.

Mr. LANGEVIN. Anybody else want to comment on the challenges?

General MOORE. Sir, I think Major General Haas covered it quite well. But if we take a look, like he said, it really depends on what area of the world we are talking about. If we want to take ISIL, for example, like we have said, their abilities using social media, using cyber capabilities is really one of their centers of gravity. And it is the speed at which you can operate, an individual person can operate, it is the depth at which they can reach into a population. They can do it 24/7, 365 days a year. And so it is how do you keep up and combat the speed at which that message may be getting out?

So it is not just about the message itself, it is also tied into the speed at which they can get that message out and they can update it.

Mr. LANGEVIN. How challenged are we with respect to the language barriers? I would imagine that this is something that we have accounted for. And I know we have folks working on developing and enhancing our linguistic capabilities. But how is that hampering our ability?

General HAAS. Where we are not fluent in a language, sir, I think the challenge is we rely on interpreters. And we train our soldiers in how to work with interpreters, but once again, it could potentially be a foreign national, or a local national that is providing that data, and therefore, it is not that individual operator who has the fluency in the language to be able to provide those recommendations, options, courses of actions for how we should do counter-propaganda. It is coming through an interpreter. So we are always working on trying to improve our language skills within our MISO community.

Mr. LANGEVIN. Good. Thank you, General. Thanks, Chairman, I yield back. Thank you for your testimony.

Mr. WILSON. Thank you, Ranking Member. And again, for each of you, we are very, very grateful for your service. You make a difference to promote a level of stability, which is so important not just for American families, but for people around the world. With this, we now conclude and we are adjourned.

[Whereupon, at 3:19 p.m., the subcommittee was adjourned.]

APPENDIX

OCTOBER 22, 2015

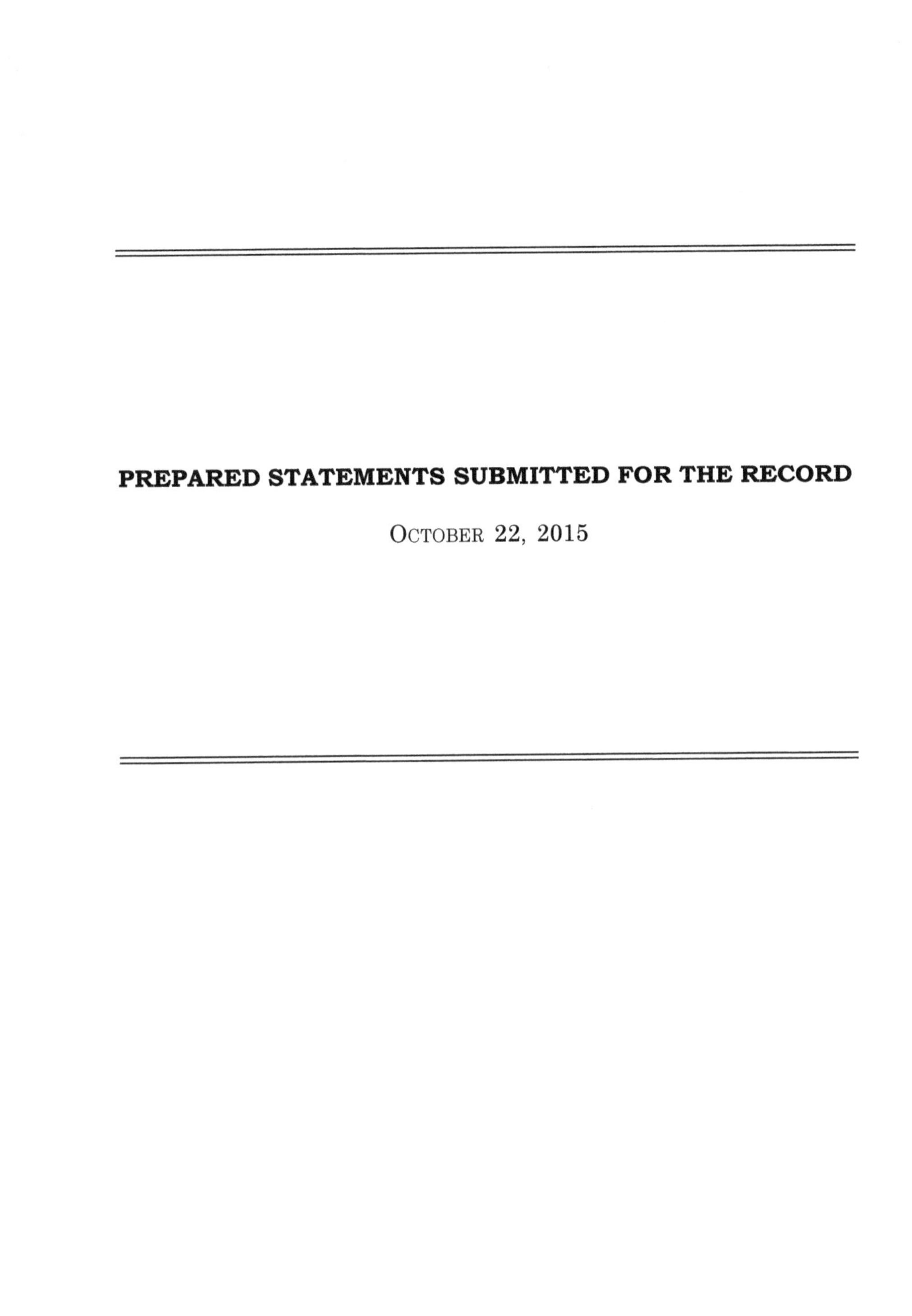

<hr>

PREPARED STATEMENTS SUBMITTED FOR THE RECORD

OCTOBER 22, 2015

<hr>

Chairman Joe Wilson Opening Statement

Countering Adversarial Propaganda: Charting an Effective Course in the Contested Information Environment

22 October 2015

Ladies and gentlemen, I call this hearing of the Emerging Threats and Capabilities subcommittee to order.

I am pleased to welcome everyone here for today's hearing on information operations and counter-propaganda capabilities. This hearing will focus on the challenges faced by the Department of Defense and the federal government when dealing with the insidious propaganda and social media messaging coming from groups like Da'esh, and countries such as Russia, China and others. Not only do they recruit members, raise money, and sway the opinions of potential allies with this propaganda, but they sow doubt and dissension as a means of preventing or discouraging U.S. action.

Last month, our subcommittee held a closed roundtable discussion with outside industry and academic experts to explore this topic. That discussion helped our members better understand some core challenges and concerns, including:

- What are our current capabilities for information operations and counter-propaganda, and how are they being integrated into larger strategies to deal with specific actors like Da'esh, Russia, Iran, China and others?

- How can new technologies and concepts improve our ability to sense, detect, analyze, and respond to propaganda in the 21st century media environment?

- What policy challenges impair our ability to realize the full potential of these new technologies and concepts?

These questions and issues remain relevant to today's hearing. Our panel of expert witnesses will proceed from that starting point, and provide us with their thoughts from a governmental perspective on this important topic.

Our witnesses before us today are:

The Honorable Michael Lumpkin
Assistant Secretary of Defense for Special Operations and Low-Intensity Conflict

The Honorable Matthew Armstrong
Broadcasting Board of Governors

(27)

Major General Christopher K. Haas
Director, Force Management and Development, United States Special
Operations Command (SOCOM)

Brigadier General Charles Moore
Deputy Director for Global Operations, Joint Staff

I'd like to turn now to my friend Mr. Jim Langevin from Rhode Island for any comments he'd like to make.

Testimony of Matthew Armstrong
Member, Broadcasting Board of Governors
Before the House Armed Services Committee, Subcommittee on Emerging
Threats and Capabilities
October 22, 2015

Mr. Chairman and Members of the Subcommittee, thank you for inviting me to speak to the unique role the Broadcasting Board of Governors (BBG) and United States international media play in advancing our national interests.

I am pleased to join today's panel alongside my colleagues from the Department of Defense (DoD). It is appropriate, and important, that we remain vigilant to the ways in which information and ideas impact our national security. Every day, around the world, we face adversaries and challengers whose primary weapon is not kinetic, but the expert deployment, and at times active suppression, of information.

In today's increasingly interconnected world, responding to the global explosion of information must be a key focus of U.S. foreign policy. Each day, the voices and messages of our friends and foes alike travel and impact beyond familiar political borders with the press of a "share" button. Communities and conversations in the digital space are created without limit to a specific geographical area. As technology continues to develop, cross-border communications and dissemination of information will only increase.

While the information revolution offers the world a plethora of opportunity, particularly those who have lacked a voice either locally and on the global stage, it also provides challenges. In just the past five years, we have seen vivid examples where both state and non-state actors have effectively used information to challenge the United States, our values of democracy and freedom, and the very existence of objective truth.

From Crimea, to Syria, Northern Nigeria, and Southeast Asia, propaganda and censorship have resurged in our increasingly networked world to foment hate and confusion, monitor and suppress dissent, activate acts of terror and roll-back hard-won freedoms. Actors from ISIL to Russia to China are using information not just to "win the news cycle," but to shape the very choices of statecraft.

U.S. foreign policy cannot be effective if we do not appreciate how information shapes the actions of policymakers, institutions, and everyday citizens on the street. The simple truth is that today's media has the power to reach through the screen to activate audiences to action – or to suppress them. Failing to recognize this fact limits the effectiveness of our foreign policy.

U.S. international media advances U.S. national interests by engaging audiences that are critical to advancing democratic values through open and free exchanges of information.

The BBG oversees all nonmilitary international media supported by the U.S. government, including the Voice of America (VOA), the Office of Cuba Broadcasting (OCB), and BBG-funded grantees Radio Free Europe/Radio Liberty, Inc. (RFE/RL), Radio Free Asia (RFA) and the Middle East Broadcasting Networks, Inc. (MBN). We inform, engage, and connect people around the world in support of freedom and democracy.

Throughout U.S. international media's long history, the tools and goals have been consistent: delivering consistently accurate, reliable and credible reporting that opens minds and stimulates debate in closed societies and those where free media are not yet fully established – especially where local media fails to inform and empower its citizens.

The mission of the Broadcasting Board of Governors is unique. We are a 24/7 global media organization, built for a global mission. BBG radio, television, Internet, and mobile programs reach more than 215 million people each week, in sixty-one languages.

As a journalism organization, our mission is to empower people with both the truth and the context of local, regional, and global affairs, as well as through news from the United States. Our journalists don't just present the news, they unpack the news to provide their audiences with a greater understanding of their world and what is happening. Great journalism – the stories that stick with an audience – shows, often indirectly and subtly, how democracies should work. Great journalism helps audiences understand how democratic accountability, rule of law (not rule by law), human rights, and human security should work, and the differences between the vision of democratic ideals and the reality, so that audiences understand the contrast.

The unique difference of the BBG is not only that we do the news in sixty-one different languages, but also that we prioritize our content to impact our strategic audiences. Many of our reporters are not only from our target markets, but they also maintain extensive networks in them and speak as locals. They don't parachute in. We know the audiences, what they need to know, and how the story is best told. This is what makes the BBG networks, including VOA, unique. We are called upon, as enshrined in our founding legislation, to operate in markets until "private information dissemination is found to be adequate." Virtually by definition, we target markets that are hard to reach and, at best, under served by accessible reliable independent media. There is no other agency or corporation like us – that puts the audience first, and that actively builds true, independent media markets, in order to one day not be needed. We use future redundancy as a primary measure of success.

President Obama said in his recent speech at the U.N. General Assembly: "The strength of nations depends on the success of their people – their knowledge, their innovation, their imagination, their creativity, their drive, their opportunity – and that, in turn, depends upon individual rights and good governance and personal security."

By unleashing the power of professional journalism, we open up new markets for independent media and, in doing so, challenge the governments, institutions, and non-state actors who would manipulate facts to limit choice or infringe the rights of their people. Accurate news not only informs the public, it allows individuals to aspire to freedom by offering them a platform from which to make decisions based on what is verifiably true – rather than on what their governments may tell them. In short, by exporting the power of a free press we fuel and sustain the exchange of ideas and the struggle for individual thought and freedom – the very building blocks of democratic freedom.

The VOA Charter, which is enshrined in our enabling legislation, mandates that our programs "present the policies of the United States clearly and effectively, and…also present responsible discussions and opinion on these policies." In this way we are a part of broader U.S. public diplomacy, a means by which the U.S. Government can articulate and explain its policies and actions, and through which Congress and other constituencies can present alternate views.

Our journalism exposes corruption and abuse, and empowers our audience to root it out. When we cover the success of free and open elections, as we have recently in Nigeria, we educate audiences on how opposition parties can seek power peacefully through the ballot. When we help repressed voices talk about their future, as we do in Iran, we show how communities can solve problems on their own.

And when we train the lens on our own challenges, for example by covering the protests surrounding Ferguson, Missouri and the subsequent national debate on racial equality, the Detroit bankruptcy, or differing views on key foreign policy initiatives, such as the recent negotiations with Iran, we allow the world to see democracy not as an abstraction, but as a constantly evolving work in progress. This reporting shows the strength of our democracy – the identification of problems, the ability to air our differences in peaceful, respectful ways in line with the rule of law – and gives the opportunity to dive into often unfamiliar concepts to our audiences, such as accountability of civil authorities, what a grand jury is, and how a legal system can work. Even talking about how – and why – Americans go about paying parking tickets can open the eyes of our audiences.

Journalism is a powerful force for change. By acting as the "foreign domestic media" we play a critical role in the lives of audiences, as a news source that provides them with information, in their local language and relevant to their daily lives, that helps them make critical decisions. Decisions on their tolerance for local corruption. Decisions on whether to believe disinformation or form an opinion on fact-based information. Decisions on whether to be connected to the world or remain isolated from it.

U.S. International Media and U.S. Foreign Policy

Today, with so much of the world awash in information, the BBG's role is changing. As our adversaries have embraced the opportunities to engage and influence audiences using new tools and techniques, the BBG has made changes as well.

Our success no longer depends on our unique global reach, but also on the intensity of the BBG's relationships with its audiences, the extent to which they share and comment on our news and information and, ultimately, how they influence local knowledge and thought.

The impact of U.S. international media for the next decade is based on our ability to be an influential news and information source in this dynamic 21st century information environment. Under the leadership of our new CEO, the BBG is aggressively moving along five core themes to be the 21st century media organization the tax payers – and the Government – demands.

First, the BBG is accelerating our shift toward engaging audiences on digital platforms, especially utilizing the power of video, mobile, and social networks. We must be on the platform, in the format, and providing the content the audience needs – be it radio, television, or mobile tools and social media. To be clear, this is not just one-way dissemination, but also the empowering and encouraging of their participation in the conversations.

Second, we are rapidly expanding coordination and content-sharing across the BBG's five interdependent networks in order to cover and report on the stories that matter to audiences and markets that increasingly transcend political borders and languages. For instance, this will allow us to more effectively share our coverage of the Middle East with interested audiences in Indonesia and Russia, or issues surrounding Chinese investment in Africa with audiences across Latin America.

Third, the BBG is concentrating its efforts in five key issue areas where we can be most effective in support of our mission. These five areas are Russia; covering violent extremism; the widening regional influence of Iran; China, not only in the South China Sea region, but also in Africa and Latin America; and, the continuing struggle for democratic rights in Cuba.

Fourth, we are evolving to an organization actively engaged in curating, commissioning, and acquiring content. This is about more than just internal capacity. There are new generations of compelling storytellers, such as the youth in many of our markets, documentarians and journalists that engage their peers every day on digital platforms.

Finally, in the past, the BBG was asked to maximize our potential reach, as befitting a broadcasting organization with a broadcasting mentality. We "paid back" the American people whenever we powered up a new transmitter or launched a new program over satellite. Today, we are focusing on impact over reach; specifically by putting the audience first in how we collect, create and distribute news and information.

Now, let me touch upon three key challenges that may be of interest to the Committee.

Responding to Russia

The Kremlin has demonstrated the use of propaganda and disinformation as a tool of foreign policy, as well as maintaining support at home. By doing so, the

Kremlin has built a house of cards that is susceptible to the truth and transparency. We see the constant statements and laws to shut down the freedom of speech and the freedom to listen in Russia. We see the same in the Kremlin's second greatest export – propaganda and obfuscation – that encourages audiences to "Question More" - to the point of not trusting anyone or thinking independently.

Countering Russian propaganda is not a proactive strategy; it is a reactionary posture predisposed to responding to the Kremlin's initiative. It allows the Kremlin the space to be proactive in disseminating disinformation to distract and obfuscate reality to manufacture blame and mask their own activities.

The BBG engages key audiences in Russia, the Russian periphery, and globally to provide them with the realities about Russian, and US activities, and, importantly, their context. Like elsewhere, we want our audiences to be empowered by facts and to think, to see the 'say-do' gaps of their leaders, which we have found over the decades to be a successful strategy for countering propaganda. For instance, RFE/RL continues to ramp up DIGIM, its new social-media driven digital reporting and engagement service, which includes the "Footage vs. Footage" feature, a daily video product that compares and contrasts how Russian media and global media report on the same events, providing the facts of a case and pointing out inconsistencies in Russian reporting.

We engage the audience's – often silently held – interests and concerns. The fundamental question that Former Soviet Union (FSU) citizens are considering is "Are we headed in the right direction?" They are weighing whether Putin's political and social reality is where they want to raise their children, start or grow a business, get an education; these are pocketbook and core questions that speak to hopes and dreams. In other words, the future media environment is not just about countering Kremlin propaganda, but a campaign for the future of the region.

<u>Covering Violent Extremism</u>

Extremist narratives too often go unaddressed within local media environments and digital echo chambers. These narratives are often tied to extremists' alleged religious virtue and organizational invincibility, with a toxic additive of anti-American conspiracy theories.

Our journalism exposes the gap between rhetoric and reality – ideologically and organizationally – of extremist groups. We do this through objective reporting that adheres to the highest standards of professional journalism. By covering violent extremism, we expose it for what it is.

Extremist groups have excelled at re-centering the news cycle on their violence. The BBG offers audiences more than coverage of violence through programming on positive alternative visions for the world to build support for more stable local and regional communities.

While other parts of the government directly support civil society, the BBG is uniquely positioned to elevate moderate voices – from the street to the elites. To cover local issues of concern, and provide constructive outlets for communities to discuss the issues that matter to them. For example, MBN's 30-minute, weekly documentary series "Delusional Paradise" presents firsthand accounts, obtained through original interviews, of families and communities that have suffered at the hands of ISIL. The program includes compelling accounts of families, in their own words, who have lost loved ones both due to ISIL recruitment and attacks, including the first interview with the Jordanian pilot's family.

Internet Freedom

A third prominent challenge for us is the fundamental importance of information freedom.

This is an enduring and central role for the BBG. Almost 75 years ago, President Roosevelt gave his 'Four Freedoms' speech that symbolized America's war aims and gave hope to a war-wearied people because they knew they were fighting for freedom. His first freedom was of speech and expression everywhere in the world.

Today information freedom means the freedom for people around the world to be informed, to engage and connect with one another and ultimately use that information to change their lives and the lives of their community for the better.

I have followed, worked on, and blogged about public diplomacy and strategic communication issues for more than a decade. And I've been privileged enough to combine these experiences in my work on the Broadcasting Board of Governors.

I recall the rush when early bloggers in formerly closed societies pushed the envelope, and blogged about things their governments would rather see kept quiet.

At the time, there were those who called blogs "the samizdat of the 21st century" – a reference to the underground newsletters self-published by Soviet dissidents during the Cold War. And, for a time, bloggers and independent journalists did do some astounding work in places like Russia, China, Iran, Cuba, Egypt and Azerbaijan.

The BBG created the Internet Anti-Censorship (or "IAC" program) to accomplish two simple goals. The first is to support journalists, bloggers, civil society actors and activists to use the Internet safely and without fear of interference. The second is empower world citizens to have access to modern communication channels that are free of restrictions, and allow them to communicate without fear of repressive censorship or surveillance.

Using funds provided by Congress for internet freedom programs, our International Broadcasting Bureau funds large scale proxy servers and other means to defeat censorship, such as proxy servers like Psiphon. Through the BBG's investment and supports of multiple circumvention technologies, we have been able to create a new generation of mobile apps that directly challenge and overcome the firewall of Iran and Great Firewall of China. Our web proxy servers allow literally over a billion sessions a day of Internet users from the Middle East, North Africa, Eurasia and East Asia to access news and information outside of their tightly controlled information markets.

Through our Open Technology Fund, we underwrite apps and programs for computers and mobile devices that help to encrypt communications and evade censorship. OTF's approach to identify and support next-generation internet freedom technologies has led to the development of first-of-its kind tools which support encryption of text messages and mobile phone calls, detection of mobile phone censorship and intrusion efforts, and technologies which allow transfer of data without use of the internet or mobile networks. Such efforts allow users facing changing methods of curtailing free expression online to continue to communicate safely.

The success of our Internet Freedom work is at the core of our role as journalists and reflects our unique capabilities within the U.S. government. In the digital era, the freedom to speak and the freedom to listen remain essential. And you can count on the BBG expanding our efforts in this area into the future.

Cooperation between BBG and Department of Defense

Finally, I would like to turn towards our engagement with other U.S. government colleagues. The BBG has a unique set of capabilities that were enabled by a range of authorities and requirements that first established and then grew U.S. international media. While we do work closely with other parts of government to accomplish our own mission, the Board of Governors and staff at the BBG remain committed to, and strong guardians of, the Agency's statutory journalistic firewall, which ensures the independence and journalistic integrity of our broadcasts and other content.

Having said this, the BBG does cooperate effectively with other U.S. government agencies, including colleagues at the Department of Defense, Department of State, USAID, and the Centers for Disease Control. We have a number of projects already underway with each agency, and are exploring others where appropriate.

The BBG has worked closely with various different DoD commands to accomplish mutual goals. In an agreement with Africa Command, the Voice of America produced a youth program to understand the impacts of violent extremism among Somalia youth. The radio programming was supplemented by SMS messaging, Town Hall meetings and journalism training for young people.

In Southeast Asia we have executed an agreement with Pacific Command that enabled the BBG to launch a new journalism effort focused on extremism in that region, including Thailand, Indonesia, Bangladesh and Malaysia.

And Voice of America continues to train broadcast technicians and photographers within the combatant commands in the technical aspects of journalism. We are already laying plans to host and train more technical operations staff during the FY 2016 fiscal year.

Conclusion

To close, the fundamental purpose and intent of the BBG is to empower our audiences to own their future. We enable this goal by providing fact-based alternatives to the propaganda they suffer, giving them access to truth, and demonstrating the building blocks of democratic society – accountability, rule of law (versus rule by law), human security issues, and more.

Voice of America's first broadcast stated: "The news may be good or bad; we will tell you the truth." At BBG, we continue to operate with that in mind, because truth builds trust and credibility, and delivering credible news is the most effective means to ensure impact and provide the audience with information that will affect their daily lives and use in their own decision-making.

And with that, I am happy to take questions. Thank you for your time and attention.

Matthew Armstrong
Broadcasting Board of Governors

Matthew C. Armstrong has been a strategist and thought leader on public diplomacy and strategic communication for about ten years. He has experience working on traditional and emerging security issues with both civilian and military agencies in the U.S. and Europe, as well as journalists and news organizations, think tanks, and academia on three continents.

In 2011, he served as executive director of the U.S. Advisory Commission on Public Diplomacy. He was an adjunct professor of public diplomacy at the Annenberg School of Journalism and Communication at the University of Southern California, founded the MountainRunner Institute, a 501(c)3 studying public diplomacy, and published a blog on public diplomacy and strategic communication. Mr. Armstrong also serves as the Secretary of the Public Diplomacy Council, is a member of the National Press Club, and sits on the editorial board of the journal of the NATO Strategic Communication Center of Excellence. He earned a Bachelor's of Arts in International Relations and a Master of Public Diplomacy from the University of Southern California.

Mr. Armstrong chairs the Special Committee on the Voice of America in the 21st Century and is a member of the Board's Advisory Committee. He also served as the chair of the Special Committee on the Future of Shortwave Broadcasting, which on August 1, 2014, issued its report, To Be Where the Audience Is; The Future of Shortwave.

He was confirmed as member of the Broadcasting Board of Governors on August 1, 2013.

Prepared Remarks for the Hon. Michael Lumpkin, ASD (SO/LIC)

Countering Adversarial Propaganda Hearing for Members of the House Armed Services Committee, Subcommittee on Emerging Threats and Capabilities

Thursday, October 22, 2:00 PM

Rayburn House Office Building, Room RHOB 2212

Introduction and the Oversight Role of ASD (SO/LIC)

Chairman Wilson, Ranking Member Langevin, and distinguished Members of the committee—I appreciate this opportunity today to discuss the Department of Defense's important supporting role to our government's efforts led by the Department of State in today's contested information environment. In advance I would like to thank you for this committee's support in this critical field. I will focus my remarks on the Department's supporting role in the U.S. Government effort and on the need to maintain agile authorities. I am very pleased to be joined today by the Brigadier General Moore, the Deputy Director for Global Operations in the Joint Staff operations directorate, to provide an operational perspective, and Major General Haas from U.S. Special Operations Command (USSOCOM), to discuss that command's role in ensuring the readiness of the Military Information Support Operations (MISO) force. I am here to discuss an aspect of our information operations capabilities that has received special attention from your committee and the other defense committees over the last few years: our military information support operations force, which provides a critical influence capability to meet the tactical and operational needs of military commands and provide support to the overall strategic effort led by the State Department. As we begin this hearing, I think it is important to note that I am not discussing the Department's Public Affairs capabilities. Public affairs is a fully separate activity from MISO and is directed at engaging the media and informing U.S. and other audiences.

As the principal civilian advisor to the Secretary of Defense on special operations and low-intensity conflict matters, I directly support the Under Secretary of Defense for Policy in her role as the Principal Staff Advisor for Information Operations (IO). Additionally, in my role as the principal special operations official within the senior management of the Department of Defense, I oversee USSOCOM in its role as the joint proponent for military information support operations. I am committed to ensuring that we develop, maintain, and employ the proper IO capabilities to meet the tactical and operational requirements of military commands and provide support to the strategic effort led by the Department of State.

The Department's Supporting Role in the U.S. Government Effort.

Our MISO capabilities are unlike most capability sets in the Department of Defense, and MISO requires additional oversight and coordination that is not typically required of other Departmental activities. Whereas lethal and destructive combat capabilities tend to belong exclusively to the Department, other U.S. Government departments and agencies, such as the Broadcasting Board of Governors and the Department of State, have capabilities, roles, and missions as part of our Government's strategic communications efforts. This substantial overlap in roles and capabilities leads leads to a need for close interagency coordination and clear delineation of the appropriate roles for each organization. This coordination is conducted within an overall U.S. Government communications and engagement framework with global audiences. Within this greater framework, the Department's MISO forces provide support to military plans and operations, unique influence planning expertise, regional knowledge, and the ability to advise, assist, and develop similar partner nation forces and organizations.

The Department fully recognizes the overarching need for a strategic, whole-of-government effort in communications efforts. The Department of State generally leads U.S. Government communications and engagement efforts focused on foreign audiences. For example, the Department of State is home to the Center for Strategic Counterterrorism Communications (CSCC), which has the mission to "coordinate, orient, and inform government-wide strategic communications focused on violent extremists and terrorist organizations." The Department of Defense's efforts alone will not solve the challenge of this contested information environment and adversary propaganda. Instead the Department of Defense plays a critical role as a contributor and partner to the whole-of-government effort led by the State Department.

The Department also recognizes the military necessity of operating in the information environment. Our combatant commanders have clear military objectives to maintain the stability and security of their regions, in concert with other U.S. Government efforts, and this involves operating in the information environment. Additionally, the Department can offer unique military capabilities that can play a critical role in achieving overall communications objectives. These types of actions are not done, or conceived, in competition with other U.S. departments and agencies but in coordination with them.

As we employ our MISO forces in environments outside areas of military hostilities, we will always maintain military command and control of our forces and operate in a manner that achieves mutual support between U.S. departments and agencies. At the national level, we will partner with the lead agency, usually the Department of State, and provide unique Defense capabilities to support the coordination and synchronization of a whole-of-government effort that combines public diplomacy, public affairs, U.S. international media, information operations, and other capabilities. At the request of the State Department, the Department has provided five military IO and MISO planners to the cell within CSCC that coordinates our national efforts against the Islamic State of Iraq and the Levant (ISIL), and we currently maintain an additional MISO planner within the State Department to support planning in other geographic areas.

Overseas, we fully acknowledge the role of Chiefs of Mission and ensure that our military operations are fully coordinated. We always ensure we provide a complementary capability, and a capability that is not duplicative with those of other departments and agencies..

The Department also builds partnerships with other U.S. Government organizations. A key initiative that has emerged over the last year has been the Department's partnership with various entities of the Broadcasting Board of Governors (BBG). Spearheaded by a pilot project at U.S. Pacific Command, our relationship with BBG exemplifies the necessary whole-of-government approach to key challenges such as countering violent extremist ideology and exposing hostile propaganda.

Tailoring an appropriate menu of Policy Authorities

There are nuanced distinctions between informing, educating, persuading, and influencing audiences using information. The Department's efforts span all of these activities depending on the specific military mission. The key question relates to the boundaries and limitations on each department or agency's role in this space. The Department needs flexibility to be able to keep up with the nature of today's transnational threats and evolving technology. This flexibility, however, will not diminish the Department's oversight of MISO. We will make certain that our operations are tied to clear military objectives contained in theater campaign or other operational plans, that all actions are fully consistent with applicable law, including the covert action statute, and that we have achieved the necessary coordination with interagency partners.

The requirements for MISO capabilities are increasingly pressing, as our adversaries and competitors, both State and non-State actors, rely heavily on propaganda to achieve their aims. This is most evident with the sophisticated and well-resourced propaganda campaigns being waged by ISIL and by the Russian Federation becoming more and more aggressive in Eastern Europe. ISIL uses information on a global scale to recruit, facilitate foreign fighter flow, finance, and gain tacit support for their violent agenda. Similarly, Russian propaganda seeks to intimidate or undermine our allies and partners outside of areas of hostilities. Many of these activities are happening online and over social media.

These trends highlight a critical role for MISO in places outside areas of hostilities, with clear military missions supporting broader, non-military U.S. Government efforts. The Department cannot address these challenges effectively by itself; instead, in a supporting role, we will partner with our interagency colleagues and provide our unique MISO capabilities as part of a whole-of-government solution. Additionally, the Department's MISO capabilities and authorities must remain agile enough to reach our target audiences through whatever their preferred form of communication; whether it is radio, television, internet, or whatever technologies emerge in the future.

As you are aware, our Military Information Support Operations programs have been an item of special congressional interest since 2010. In the past, the MISO communities saw their budgets and authorities grow in support of Operations IRAQI and ENDURING FREEDOM. These growing budgets and their associated activities resulted in increasing concerns over their scope, effectiveness, command and control, and integration with other U.S. efforts. The Department has a clear role for MISO to change the behavior of appropriate foreign target audiences through dissemination of information tailored to influence in support of military objectives. We have endeavored to ensure we stay within this role, and we appreciate the Committee's support.

Over the past five years, the Department has worked closely with the Congress to improve and institutionalize appropriate oversight of this mission area. We have endeavored to address congressional concerns fully in this area while improving our capabilities to meet current challenges. My Information Operations

Directorate, which enables our effective oversight, is one of the largest directorates in my organization. Over the last five years, we have emplaced improved fiscal controls and scoped our budget requests to ensure a clear and direct linkage from strategy to task to resource. We have made positive strides in the area of oversight, and we appreciate the increasingly positive language and support over the last year from this Committee and others that reflects increased confidence in our oversight.

We also understand the concerns that have arisen in the past regarding the scope and effectiveness of some programs that we have since terminated. We appreciate the Committee's support in this effort. I would ask your continued support for the Department's role in this critical space, especially as we craft new programs that are threat-based, scoped to critical audiences, and developed with clear measures of effectiveness that reflect their support of military objectives and the overall State Department's-led strategic effort.

Building the future force

The imperative to stay abreast of increasing technological change and our adversaries' rapid adaptation of technology demands that the Department use a thoughtful, strategic approach to achieve success against a mix of adversaries. Simply trying to match our adversaries "tweet" for "tweet" or matching website for website would be both fiscally irresponsible and operationally ineffective. Instead, the Department must rely on the skills of its human capital to develop thoughtful, well-constructed plans and partnerships with other U.S. Government departments and agencies and with foreign partners, and to leverage a variety of means to disrupt the adversary's narrative, expose its contradictions and falsehoods, and ultimately bring credible, persuasive, and truthful information to audiences who often have significantly differing perceptions and cultural norms than our own. The Department is currently evaluating whether we are appropriately leveraging a range of emerging technologies to the maximum extent possible to gain an advantage over our adversaries.

As the Office of the Secretary of Defense exercises our oversight role, we will develop the future MISO force using the following general guidance:
First and foremost, we will continue to ensure the proper military command and control and effective organizations for our operations. Having clear military command and control linkages helps ensure synchronization and mutual support

between the range of activities by each combatant command and its subordinate components. The continual evolution of communications technology will likely require additional organizational innovation as we seek to maintain our capability to influence in an "always-on," dynamic, and interactive social media environment.

Second, we will ensure that the Department's operations in this arena are focused on designated threat groups and adversaries or support military-to-military engagement. Information activities broadly directed at large global or regional audiences are more appropriately conducted by Public Diplomacy, Public Affairs, and the BBG's media activities.

Third, we will seek the right balance between military, government civilian, and contracted capabilities. We know most of our information activities will require long-term effort. As technology and the way society utilizes the emerging communications means continue to evolve, we foresee the continual need to bring new skill sets into our MISO force.

Fourth, we will continue to maintain and build upon the partnerships we have created with our interagency partners. We will sustain the high level of trust and cooperation we already have built in support of Department of State-led efforts.

Fifth, we will seek to apply greater interagency support to our operations to ensure our operations are focused and to provide better assessment of their effectiveness.

Finally, we will continue to demonstrate the strength of our oversight and the transparency in our reporting to the congressional defense committees. We will develop and apply the right metrics and continue to bring our candid assessment back to you as to what has worked and what lessons we have learned.

Ultimately, the concepts we bring forward to you will be clearly linked with intelligence analysis and demonstrate how we will respond and defeat threats in the information environment, using greater precision and rigor in our planning. In this sense, our future planning should be similar in scope and detail to what our other special operations forces do in their counterterrorism missions.

Conclusion

In response to congressional concerns over the last six years, we have emplaced the right team and processes to provide oversight of the Department's MISO force. We recognize that even in support to military operations in areas of hostilities, the

Department's capabilities and activities must be coordinated with a strategic U.S. Government effort that is led by the Department of State. Within this role, the Department will seek to maintain agile authorities as technologies evolve and our adversaries adapt. Furthermore, we will continue to develop our forces to be proficient in the current and projected communication environment. Thank you for your support, and I pledge to ensure our MISO capabilities will be ready to play their vital role in support of commanders and their operations and as an integral part of our Nation's comprehensive efforts to counter adversary propaganda.

Michael D. Lumpkin
Assistant Secretary of Defense for Special Operations/Low-Intensity Conflict

Michael D. Lumpkin is currently the Assistant Secretary of Defense for Special Operations/Low-Intensity Conflict (SO/LIC). Mr. Lumpkin was sworn in as the Assistant Secretary of Defense for Special Operations/Low-Intensity Conflict (SO/LIC) on December 2, 2013, following his nomination by President Barack Obama and confirmation by the U.S. Senate.

In his role as Assistant Secretary (SO/LIC), Mr. Lumpkin is the principal advisor to the U.S. Secretary of Defense on Special Operations and Low Intensity Conflict. He is responsible primarily for the overall supervision, to include oversight of policy and resources, of special operations and low intensity conflict activities. These activities include: counterterrorism, unconventional warfare, direct action, special reconnaissance, foreign internal defense, civil affairs, information operations, and counter-proliferation of weapons of mass destruction. In his role as Assistant Secretary (SO/LIC), Mr. Lumpkin also oversees the Department of Defense counter-narcotics program, building partnership capacity initiatives and humanitarian and disaster relief efforts.

Prior to his assuming duties as Assistant Secretary (SO/LIC), Mr. Lumpkin served as a Senior Executive at both the Department of Defense and Department of Veterans Affairs. His previous positions include Special Assistant to the Secretary of Defense, Principal Deputy Assistant Secretary of Defense for (SO/LIC), and Deputy Chief of Staff for Operations at the Department of Veterans Affairs.

Mr. Lumpkin has also significant experience in the private sector where he served as the Chief Executive Officer (CEO) at Industrial Security Alliance Partners and Executive Director of Business Development at ATI.

Mr. Lumpkin has more than 20 years of active duty military service as a US Navy SEAL where he held every leadership position from platoon commander to Team commanding officer. Mr. Lumpkin has participated in numerous campaigns and contingencies throughout the world to include both Operations Iraqi Freedom and Enduring Freedom.

Mr. Lumpkin holds a MA from Naval Postgraduate School in National Security Affairs. He is a recognized subspecialist in Special Operations/Low-Intensity Conflict and Western Hemisphere Affairs.

PREPARED STATEMENT

OF

MG CHRISTOPHER HAAS

U.S SPECIAL OPERATIONS COMMAND
DIRECTOR, DIRECTORATE OF FORCE MANAGEMENT AND DEVELOPMENT

BEFORE THE
HOUSE ARMED SERVICES COMMITTEE
EMERGING THREATS AND CAPABILITIES SUBCOMMITTEE

OCTOBER 22, 2015

INTRODUCTION

Mr. Chairman, and distinguished Members of the committee, thank you for the opportunity to come before you today to discuss US Special Operations Command's (USSOCOM) manning, training, and equipping of the Military Information Support Operations (MISO) force. While I will cover the broader aspects of each of those responsibilities, I will comment from a perspective of countering our adversaries' influence efforts. Preparing our MISO forces for current and future conflict is a critical role for USSOCOM. The USSOCOM Commander places a great deal of emphasis on operating in the human domain, which is particularly important in our current conflicts and is the focus of our MISO forces. As Assistant Secretary of Defense Lumpkin previously mentioned, the extensive propaganda efforts employed by both the Islamic State of Iraq and the Levant (ISIL) and the Russian Federation make USSOCOM's role in manning, training and equipping the MISO force even more critical. We have made significant improvements in all three areas over the last decade, but there is considerable work remaining—particularly in improving our MISO force's capability through training to counter our adversaries' influence on the world-wide web which they currently extensively exploit.

MANNING THE MISO FORCE TO OPTIMIZE ITS IMPACT

The first of USSOCOM's roles is to adequately man the MISO force. Without the right number of skilled people in the right positions, the MISO force cannot accomplish its mission. Overall end strength of the two active duty groups is 1051 officers and enlisted MISO Soldiers. The active MISO officer corps is 224 assigned against 204 billets and is appropriately manned at the Captain, Lieutenant Colonel and Colonel levels. The aggregate strength of the active duty officer force is 112 percent, which is comparable to other branches. This end strength will be adjusted by management tools such as selected early retirement, and promotion reductions. The majorities of officers are serving at the operational level (55%) and at Special Operations Forces commands (16%). Our noncommissioned officers are also appropriately manned at the Staff Sergeant or E-6 levels and above; however, the inventory of Sergeants (E-5) is below authorized levels. The strength of our active duty groups' enlisted force is 872 assigned against 1295 billets, a shortage of 423 Soldiers.

The total active duty officer and enlisted strength is 70 percent, with more than 88 percent serving at the operational level. While this is not an ideal situation at the enlisted level, our projections indicate the training pipeline should have active duty MISO groups fully manned by FY 2019. Also, our FY2015 retention statistics indicate that retention efforts for the two active duty groups are retaining enough quality personnel to avoid any degradation to their current capabilities. The United States Army John F. Kennedy Special Warfare Center and School is exploring additional opportunities through the Army Special Operations Forces Recruiting Battalion to recruit more Officer and NCO candidates. These opportunities include possible retention incentives targeting enlisted Soldiers in the ranks of sergeant to sergeant first class with qualifying language scores. Additionally, the active duty groups are participating in recruiting events with the Army Special Operations Recruiting Battalion that are specifically targeted to increase the number of officer and enlisted candidates for MISO selection and assessment.

An additional aspect of manning the force is placing personnel in an optimum force structure. In 2014, the United States Army Special Operations Command re-organized the United States Special Forces Command from exclusively manning, training and equipping Special Forces units

to now include Civil Affairs and the two active duty MISO Groups. This streamlining of effort,
now represents the largest, newest and most adaptive Army Division providing the Geographic
Combatant Commanders and Theater Special Operations Commanders the forces necessary to
accomplish their assigned missions. This command relationship has already provided synergy to
operations in AFRICOM, CENTCOM and EUCOM areas of responsibility, such as with
operations against Joseph Kony and the Lord's Resistance Army in Central Africa where MISO,
Special Forces and Civil Affairs elements have enabled partner nation efforts resulting in
dramatic gains in combating this adversary.

TRAINING THE MISO FORCE – ADAPTING TO THE MISSION

The complexity of mission and the expertise required to carry out MISO missions has shaped
and extended the training program for MISO soldiers. Prior to any formal training, service
members seeking to enter the MISO force undergo an extensive selection process— a process
designed to identify those able to function under physical and mental stress. Assessment and
selection is a ten-day process with eight selection cycles per year. All candidates are assessed
against the core SOF attributes—integrity, courage, perseverance, personal responsibility,
professionalism, adaptability, teamwork, and capability, as well as validated physical and mental
occupational performance standards. All events are designed to measure specific attributes
required to posture a candidate for success in the MISO field. Candidates are isolated and
undergo both physical and mental stressors to measure problem solving abilities, resilience and
stamina.

Following selection into the MISO career field, our Soldiers attend a 5-phase, 42-week
training program. This training includes extensive studies in MISO planning, linguistics, and
cultural knowledge, interagency support, media development and dissemination, effective

analysis and assessments and translator/interpreter management. The end state of the training pipeline is to produce a skilled MISO soldier capable of planning, executing and measuring MISO across the full spectrum of operations in all environments in support of joint, interagency, multinational or coalition operations. These soldiers are capable of operating in both technologically superior and austere environments. They are responsive and adaptive to asymmetrical challenges; adaptive and comfortable with ambiguity. They are culturally aware, regionally focused and language-capable. Two areas of this MISO training that differentiate them from other US Government capabilities are the focus on language and culture as well as a focus on influence principles. I'd like to highlight these two unique characteristics. The language and cultural priorities are based upon MISO force demand and are oriented on critical regions of the world. While it can be challenging to produce fluent language speakers in many of the more challenging languages, the benefits of understanding language and culture are critical in determining how a culture communicates or the value a culture places on relationships. These shared assumptions drive meaning within any group. Linguistic and cultural knowledge provide an insight which is critical to conducting effective influence operations. The extensive training that our Soldiers receive enables them to leverage the cultural nuances of influence. They learn when it is most appropriate to use an emotional appeal or a rational argument, what the best mix of media is to convey a certain type of argument, and what symbols are relevant in conveying the specific message. This training, combined with linguistic and cultural understanding, makes MISO a true SOF capability and a distinct asset within the Department of Defense. In regards to training volume, in FY14 and FY15, our training base has maintained an 80 percent graduation rate.

As you well know, our adversaries use the Internet to contact and recruit followers, gain financial support and to spread propaganda and misinformation. As I mentioned in my introduction, we continue to adapt to emerging requirements. The current conflicts have identified that we have a need to continue expanding our MISO training, primarily with regards to the Web. Through the Joint requirements process, USCentral, USPacific, USAfrican, and USEuropean Commands all identified gaps in regard to MISO use of the Web. SOCOM is in the process of developing a comprehensive plan capturing all aspects of this requirement; a key aspect of the requirement being training. This training will incorporate social media use, online advertising, web metrics, and web design, among many other topics. Such a training solution will also enable us to stop being so dependent upon a contracted solution. In the interest of managing expectations however, such training cannot happen overnight and we may always need some level of contracted support in translation and IT expertise. We will be dependent upon contractors in the short term as we train the force. While this occurs we will seek to accomplish significant on the job training and learning from the contracted expertise to augment our training efforts. Ultimately, we will find the right balance between what tasks the MISO force can execute and those requiring contracted expertise to accomplish.

EQUIPPING THE MISO FORCE – STAYING CURRENT

Maintaining a current MISO equipment capability to meet operational requirements is an ongoing effort, but one USSOCOM is well positioned to meet. We have been upgrading our MISO production and dissemination capability continuously to meet the force's requirements. We have a state-of-the-art Media Production Center at Fort Bragg, with the capability to provide for print, audio, and video product development. The Center also includes redundant archival features to preserve all past and current MISO planning and production efforts. Some of the current deployable equipment includes: the flyaway broadcast system, a radio, TV, and cellular broadcast capability, next generation loudspeaker systems, and an interoperable responsive short or long term mass printing capability. These systems are fielded and in operation by our MISO forces supporting commands around the world.

We are also constantly exploring and developing future MISO capabilities to ensure we meet the emerging needs of the Geographic Combatant Commands and Theater Special Operations Commands. This process involves researching emerging technologies, assessing the needs of the MISO force, and MISO systems development, with integrated testing and evaluation. All equipment decisions are made in accordance with the USSOCOM Commander's prioritized resourcing guidance, developed from an objective mission and gap analysis of USSOCOM mission sets. Some of the future capabilities we are in the process of developing are the distributable audio media system, a leaflet-like system with embedded pre-recorded audio and/or audio-visual messages, an upgraded version of the flyaway broadcast system mentioned earlier with a 97% size/weight reduction, and the long range broadcast system; a pod-mounted radio, TV, and cellular broadcast system on manned and unmanned aircraft allowing MISO message broadcast out to 100 miles. We are also in the process of testing an Internet Production Capability (IPC), which will be a fully integrated suite of work stations designed to perform web research, data capture, message product development, and web-based message delivery. The IPC will provide a secure means of navigating the Web, a means to conduct social media analysis, provide multiple methods to deliver online messages, and provide the ability to monitor real-time measures of effectiveness and adjust MISO programs/campaigns shortly after launching on social media.

USSOCOM welcomes the committee's support regarding technology demonstrations to assess innovative, new technologies for MISO. This is timely in light of the previously mentioned comprehensive plan USSOCOM is developing to address the Geographic Combatant Command gaps regarding MISO use of the Web. This plan will include a detailed analysis of the equipment component as part of the solution. Such analysis will address what equipment is needed in various locations to support operations. Congressional support will greatly assist in jump-starting that aspect of the plan and will ensure our force remains current and is able to accomplish assigned missions in support of our National Security objectives. While we will develop detailed plans, the web-based technologies we are exploring are less reliant on home station basing and more flexible in nature to provide support on-site to the Geographic Combatant Commands and Theater Special Operations Commands and reflect our commitment to providing MISO support to the Geographic Combatant Commands.

CONCLUSIONS

In conclusion, once again I would like to thank the committee members for the opportunity to provide information in regard to USSOCOM's role in manning, training and equipping its MISO force. USSOCOM stands ready to counter our adversaries in any environment, including the information environment. All shortfalls are being addressed and mitigated through the creative and adaptive use of current personnel and equipment, leveraging contracted services and personnel where appropriate. Our MISO forces monitor, assess and evaluate media trends in the information environment. We recognize the importance of operating in this space and believe we clearly have a role of engaging on the worldwide web focused specifically on the threat in support of military objectives as part of the whole-of-government approach. The mission is challenging – the information environment moves faster than ever before and supporting technology evolves at an even faster pace. Our adversaries are currently using propaganda and misinformation to great effect, often with a mix of sophisticated technology and overt brutality. This trend will not be deterred, and will only accelerate if not contested. It is a safe assumption that future adversaries will observe, learn, and adapt new strategies. We must move forward with clarity of purpose and focus our uniquely qualified non-kinetic resources to combat our nation's enemies.

I also thank you for your continued support of our SOF personnel and their families; the tremendous demands we have placed upon them requires a continued commitment to provide for their well-being and support their mission success.

Major General Christopher K. Haas
Director of Force Management and Development,
United States Special Operations Command

Major General Christopher Haas graduated from Duquesne University in 1985 and was commissioned a 2nd Lieutenant of Infantry. He currently serves as the Director of Force Management and Development, United States Special Operations Command, MacDill AFB, FL.

He has attended the Infantry Officer's Basic and Advanced Courses, Airborne and Ranger Schools, the Special Forces Qualification Course, the U.S. Army Command and General Staff College and the U.S. Army war College. He also has Master of Science and Administration Degree in General Studies from the U.S Army Command and General Staff College and a Master of Science Degree in Strategic Studies from the U.S. Army War College.

His early assignments include being a rifle platoon leader in 3d Battalion, 41st Infantry Regiment, 2d Armored Division in both Germany and Fort Hood, TX; and he commanded a Special Forces Detachment–Alpha and two Companies in 5th Special Forces Group (Airborne), Fort Campbell, KY.

MG Haas commanded the 1st Battalion, 5th Special Forces Group (Airborne) at Fort Campbell, KY and was later the deputy commander of the Group. As a Colonel, he commanded the 3d Special Forces Group (Airborne) at Fort Bragg, NC and the Combined Joint Special Operations Task Force – Afghanistan. As a general officer, he has commanded Special Operations Command, United States Africa Command, Kelly Barracks, Germany; Combined Forces Special Operations Command - Afghanistan, and the U.S. Army Special Forces Command (Airborne) at Fort Bragg, NC. He also served as the Deputy Commander of U.S. Army Special Operations Command at Fort Bragg.

His staff assignments include being a battalion operations officer in 5th Special Forces Group (Airborne); Observer/Controller at the Joint Readiness Training Center, Fort Polk, LA; operations officer, later chief, Operational Support Branch, Special Operations Division, Operations Directorate, J-3, Joint Staff, Washington, DC. He also served as director of operations, J-3, Special Operations Command Central, U.S. Central Command, MacDill Air Force Base, FL, and director, legislative affairs, U.S. Special Operations Command, MacDill AFB, FL

His combat tours include OPERATIONS DESERT SHIELD/STORM in Saudi Arabia; OPERATION ENDURING FREEDOM in Afghanistan in 2001, 2006, 2008, and 2012, and OPERATION IRAQI FREEDOM in Iraq in 2003.

Testimony

Before the House Subcommittee on Emerging Threats and Capabilities

Witness Statement of

Brig Gen Charles Moore

Deputy Director for Global Operations

Joint Staff

October 22, 2015

Mr. Chairman, Ranking member, and distinguished members of the committee, thank you for the opportunity to appear before you today to discuss the actions we in the Department of Defense are taking to counter the propaganda campaigns of our adversaries.

In order to effectively achieve our military objectives and end states, Information Operations MUST be inherently integrated with all military plans and activities in order to influence and ultimately alter the behavior of our adversaries and their supporters. Simultaneously, we must defend ourselves and friends from the influence operations undertaken by our enemies. Recent events in the CENTCOM and EUCOM regions demonstrate how ISIL and Russia are using IO campaigns to influence, shape, and define the conflict. Both of these actors possess the resources and organizational structure to operate effectively in the information environment. In regards to ISIL, we assess that this organization utilizes the information domain to recruit, fund, spread their ideology and control their operations. With respect to Russia, we have seen the employment of "hybrid warfare" (which includes regular, irregular, and aggressive information operations actions) to illegally seize Crimea, foment separatist fever in several sovereign nations, and conduct operations in Syria.

There are several capabilities available to Combatant Commanders that help to achieve our objectives while minimizing the effects of enemy Information Operations and propaganda. But, the most common is the employment of our Military Information Support Operations forces or MISO forces. MISO personnel have the training and cultural understanding required to assess hostile propaganda activities and propose unique solutions that directly support our ability to achieve our military objectives.

MISO forces, operating from a U.S. Embassy, an operational task force, or a component headquarters are employed to execute DoD missions that support: named operations, geographic combatant commander (GCC) Theater Security Cooperation efforts, and public diplomacy. How Combatant Commanders employ their military information operations capabilities, to counter adversarial propaganda, is what I understand you want to focus our discussions on today.

MISO forces are currently deployed to locations around the globe, working closely with other U.S. Government departments, agencies and partner nations to address threats specific to their regions. For example, MISO forces are currently deployed to 21 U.S. embassies, working with country teams and interagency partners to challenge adversary IO actions and support broader U.S. government actions and goals. MISO forces, along with other advise and assist efforts, conduct training with some of our closest partners in order to make them more capable of conducting their own operations. Finally, our MISO forces use a variety of mediums (for example: cyber, print, TV, and radio) to disseminate information in a manner that will change perceptions and subsequently the behavior of the target audiences.

Unfortunately, as this is an unclassified hearing, the specific examples I can discuss are limited. But, I do want to provide some brief examples of the efforts our MISO forces are currently undertaking around the world.

In Central Command, MISO efforts are focused on challenging the actions of Violent Extremist organizations. For example, in Iraq, MISO forces are conducting an advise and assist role to help Iraqi forces learn how to develop indigenous Military Information Support

Operations and counter-propaganda activities. Central Command's online influence strategy is used to counter adversary narratives, shape conditions in their AOR, and to message specific target audiences. These operations include using existing web and social media platforms to support military objectives by shaping perceptions. For example, Central Command is active on Facebook, Twitter, YouTube and other online communications platforms for its Middle Eastern and Central Asian audiences; using these forums to highlight ISIL atrocities, coalition responses to ISIL activities and to highlight Coalition successes. They remain vigilant and stand ready to adapt and reshape their approach as new dissemination platforms potentially emerge.

European Command's efforts include exposing Russian mistruths and their concerted efforts to mislead European audiences as to their true intentions. We are in the final stages of staffing the European Reassurance MISO Program (ERMP), which will provide expanded authorities to conduct MISO training and in some cases, messaging support, to our partners in the region. Additionally, EUCOM is preparing to launch a pilot program in 2016 that will leverage social media to deliver information to critical target audiences. EUCOM is also looking to expand its partnership with the Broadcasting Board of Governors to further improve its information dissemination capabilities.

Pacific Command has already expanded their partnership with the Broadcasting Board of Governors to develop a new initiative that expands existing BBG counterterrorism efforts. This initiative, named BenarNews.org, was designed to address the gap left by the termination of PACOM's counterterrorism websites. Pacific Command is synchronizing a holistic counterterrorism effort consisting of BenarNews, interactive internet activities which target specific enemy actors, on line military magazines, and Military Information Support Teams.

The bottom line is that regardless of the region of the world or the enemies that we face, the DoD understands the criticality of countering an adversary's and their supporters' confidence, conviction, will and decision making while shaping behaviors supportive of our military objectives. We understand that these actions must be taken while not exceeding the authorities we have been granted and while always operating within the boundaries the Department has been given and with close coordination among our interagency partners.

Finally, I also want to express my appreciation for the support this committee has given acknowledging DoD's need to operate "across all available media to most effectively reach target audiences" and for your unwavering support of our men and women in uniform.

Thank you again for the opportunity to appear this afternoon, I look forward to answering your questions.

Brigadier General Charles L. Moore, Jr.
Joint Chiefs of Staff, J-39

Brig. Gen. Charles L. Moore, Jr. is the Deputy Director, Global Operations (J-39). He serves as the Joint Staff focal point for information operations, military information support operations, cyber operations, electronic warfare, special technical operations, and sensitive DOD support to government agencies.

General Moore was commissioned in 1989 after graduating from the U.S. Air Force Academy. He has served as an F-16 fighter pilot, instructor pilot, weapons officer, forward air controller, and instructor at the U.S. Air Force Fighter Weapons School, Nellis AFB, Nev. His command experience includes: the 555th Fighter Squadron at Aviano Air Base Italy, the 332nd Expeditionary Operations Group at Balad AB Iraq, the 20th Fighter Wing at Shaw AFB, S.C. and the 57th Wing at Nellis AFB Nev.

General Moore is a command pilot with more than 3,000 hours in the F-16 and more than 640 hours of combat time.

EDUCATION
1989 Bachelor of Science, U.S. Air Force Academy, Colo.
1995 Squadron Officer School, Maxwell AFB, Ala.
1999 Masters of Human Resource Management, Troy State University
2002 Masters of Military Operational Art/Science, Air Command and Staff College, Maxwell AFB, Ala.
2004 Air War College, by correspondence
2006 Air Force National Defense Fellow, Weatherhead Center for International Affairs, Harvard University
2011 Executive Leadership Seminar, Darden School of Business, University of Virginia
2012 Joint Forces Air Component Commander Course, Maxwell AFB, Ala.
2013 Executive Space Operations Course, Nellis AFB, Nev.

ASSIGNMENTS
1. November 1989 - March 1991, Student, Undergraduate Euro-NATO Joint Jet Pilot Training, Sheppard AFB, Texas
2. April 1991 - October 1991, Student, F-16 Replacement Training Unit, 314th Fighter Squadron, Luke AFB, Ariz.
3. October 1991 - August 1992, F-16 Pilot, Assistant Weapons Officer, 314th FS, Luke AFB, Ariz.
4. September 1992 - January 1994, F-16 Pilot, 78th Fighter Squadron, Shaw AFB, S.C.
5. January 1994 - January 1997, F-16 Instructor Pilot, Wing Electronic Combat Pilot, 20th Operations Group, Shaw AFB, S.C.
6. January 1997 - February 1998, F-16 Pilot and Weapons Officer, 35th Fighter Squadron, Kunsan AB, South Korea
7. February 1998 - August 2001, F-16 Instructor Pilot, Assistant Operations Officer, U.S. Air Force Weapons School, Nellis AFB, Nev.
8. June 2002 - June 2004, F-35/JSF Program Capabilities and Requirements Manager, Headquarters AF/XORC
9. June 2004 - July 2006, F-16 Pilot, Operations Officer, and Commander, 555th Fighter Squadron, Aviano AB, Italy
10. June 2007 - June 2008, Commander, 332nd Expeditionary Operations Group, Balad AB, Iraq
11. July 2008 - June 2010, Headquarters NORAD Vice Director of Operations, Peterson AFB, Colo.
12. June 2010 - March 2012, Commander, 20th Fighter Wing, Shaw AFB, S.C.
13. April 2012 - March 2014, Commander, 57th Wing, Nellis AFB, NV
14. March 2014 - July 2014, Chief of Security Assistance, Office of Security Cooperation-Iraq, Baghdad, Iraq
15. July 2014 - March 2015, Deputy Chief, Office of Security Cooperation-Iraq, Baghdad, Iraq
16. March 2015 - present, Deputy Director, Global Operations (J39), J-3, the Joint Staff, the Pentagon, Washington, D.C.

SUMMARY OF JOINT ASSIGNMENTS
1. July 2008 - June 2010, Headquarters NORAD Vice Director of Operations, Peterson AFB, Colo., as a colonel
2. March 2014 - present, Chief of Security Assistance and Deputy Chief, Office of Security Cooperation -- Iraq, U.S. Embassy, Baghdad, Iraq, as a brigadier general
3. March 2015 - present, Deputy Director, Global Operations (J39), J-3, the Joint Staff, the Pentagon, Washington, D.C., as a brigadier general

FLIGHT INFORMATION
Rating: command pilot
Flight hours: more than 3,000
Aircraft flown: T-37, T-38, AT-38, F-16 Blocks 30/40/50, F-15C, F-15E, F-18, B-1, B-52, HH-60, MQ-1, MQ-9

MAJOR AWARDS AND DECORATIONS
Defense Superior Service Medal with oak leaf cluster
Bronze Star
Legion of Merit with one oak leaf cluster
Meritorious Service Medal with three oak leaf clusters
Air Medal with seven oak leaf clusters
Aerial Achievement Medal with two oak leaf clusters
Air Force Commendation Medal
Air Force Achievement Medal
Joint Meritorious Unit Award with Gold Border
Meritorious Unit Award
Air Force Outstanding Unit Award with three oak leaf clusters
Air Force Organizational Excellence Award
Combat Readiness Medal
National Defense Service Medal with bronze star
Southwest Asia Service Medal with bronze star
Afghanistan Campaign Medal with bronze star
Iraq Campaign Medal with two bronze stars
Global War on Terrorism Service Medal
Korean Defense Service Medal

OTHER ACHIEVEMENTS
1990 Distinguished graduate, Undergraduate Pilot Training
1991 Distinguished graduate, F-16 RTU
1995 Distinguished graduate, Squadron Officer School
1996 Distinguished graduate/outstanding graduate, U.S. Air Force Weapons School
2005 Commander, USAFE Fighter Squadron of the Year
2007 Clarence H. Mackay Trophy

EFFECTIVE DATES OF PROMOTION
Second Lieutenant May 31, 1989
First Lieutenant May 31, 1991
Captain May 31, 1993
Major April 1, 1998
Lieutenant Colonel March 1, 2003
Colonel Jan. 1, 2007
Brigadier General Nov. 2, 2012

(Current as of April 2015)

QUESTIONS SUBMITTED BY MEMBERS POST HEARING

October 22, 2015

Mr. WILSON. How can COCOMs (and the United States Government in general, including DHS, Treasury, and State) better utilize BBG's unique pathways to and relationships with audiences?

Mr. ARMSTRONG. The BBG's reach—226 million according to Gallup research—is indeed significant.

BBG broadcasters routinely cover all major press availabilities at the Pentagon and Department of State, and we have positive relationships with senior State and DOD leaders.

That said, we continue to explore ways to expand cooperation.

We work with DHS representatives through various inter-agency processes, and find DHS material on such topics as online recruiting useful material for our programs.

We thank for the committee on their past support to revise the Smith-Mundt Act and permit domestic access to BBG content. Our content is easily accessible online. However, internal BBG procedures and (possible over-reliance on) the use of licensed content from AP and others, result in barriers for domestic media from reusing our content for rebroadcast. DHS and other inter-agency partners can promote our language services to specific immigrant communities, especially those underserved by reliable media.

BBG receives regular updates on Treasury additions and deletions to sanctions listings, and we find them particularly useful regarding Iran. The listings provide story leads, especially involving sanctions violations and financing of sanctioned organizations.

There are no regular, systematic meetings between BBG, DHS, and Treasury, however, and the idea bears consideration.

Concerning the COCOMs, the BBG and Department of Defense have a generally positive working relationship.

SOCOM's Washington office acts as one of the principle gateways between DOD and the BBG. SOCOM facilitates rotation of videographers and technicians from Ft. Bragg through short-term assignments at the Voice of America. Soldiers have the opportunity to cover spot news in the Washington area and assist in story editing and production techniques.

MIST deploying overseas typically visit BBG prior to deployment, where they receive assessments of the information and political environment. They often receive the latest audience research and public opinion studies from our Research Department.

And when they want to know about media consumption habits in the target countries, we are more than happy to share our data.

There is often technical collaboration as well. For example, BBG contributed both equipment and engineering expertise to SOCOM and other DOD elements helping to rebuild Ukraine's heavily damaged broadcast infrastructure.

BBG also contributed surplus broadcast equipment to National Guard units working to create the next-generation quick-deployment broadcast systems.

We have worked with PACOM in the creation of a dedicated, special interest digital platform, BenarNews.

This website replaces the former Khabar web site funded through the Trans Regional Web Initiative (TRWI). Funded by PACOM, BenarNews is managed and edited through BBG grantee Radio Free Asia.

The result is a content-rich site that covers a number of Asian countries—Indonesia, Malaysia, Thailand and India—which have been the subject of intense online recruiting efforts by Daesh.

We have had discussions with CENTCOM, EUCOM and AFRICOM regarding similar collaborations; those talks continue.

Working with contracting support from DOD's Countering Terrorism Technical Support Office (CTTSO), we created a prototype of a Content Exchange Platform. This digital platform would allow for easy exchange of content between various parts of the USG working on anti-Daesh and related efforts.

We believe there is merit in continuing the development efforts, as resources permit.

Mr. WILSON. How do BBG and CSCC work together? Would you make any recommendations for improving that working relationship?

Mr. ARMSTRONG. BBG works routinely with CSCC. We provide a five-days-a-week digest of BBG coverage of Daesh and related issues to CSCC, which is then distributed to USG communicators along with CSCC's daily thematic guidance.

We are also a participant in the inter-agency effort on Line of Effort #6: Demonstrating ISIL's True Nature, and we work with NCTC on Line of Effort 7: Impeding the Flow of Foreign Fighters.

As for areas of improvement, BBG is somewhat impeded by the fact that it does not have ready access to the classified e-mail systems on which much of NSCC and CSCC's business is conducted. I have been pushing for our senior leadership, especially our strategists, to get high-side accounts. At present, I am the only Governor and only one of a few individuals with a high-side account, plus one person designated as the "drop box" for receiving and sending classified email on behalf of others.

In addition, much of the work product of these organizations would provide rich content for news reports if it could be safely and expeditiously declassified.

Mr. WILSON. The U.S. must have counter propaganda with a credible voice, and do so proactively rather than reactively. a) How can we improve our own credibility? b) How can we amplify the voices of other trusted messengers? c) How do we expose the adversary's propaganda for what it is, whether from non-state or state actors? How can we engage foreign audiences to do the same? d) How can the interagency move to a proactive posture, rather than reactive, to counter messaging?

Mr. ARMSTRONG. The nature of credibility has changed in the digital age. Even in highly filtered markets bombarded by domestic and foreign propaganda, audiences can access more sources of information. As a result, they often spend less time deliberating information and may select sources that conform to their personal bias. This increased competition for attention means the BBG must focus on being relevant to the audience. Our credibility stems from being accessible in the local language, using the local vernacular, being available on the platforms the audience use (i.e. radio, TV, mobile, Internet, or print) and providing verifiable and timely news and information the audience can use. Professional journalism goes beyond simply conveying facts; it also teaches the audience how to weight the different sides.

In broader terms, the U.S. must understand that actions and words communicate and shape opinions. Often, it is the action that wins over the words. Where there is a "say-do gap," our credibility suffers. This problem is magnified where our audiences have long memories. Perhaps worse, such gaps pose potential opportunities for adversarial propaganda by our opponents.

As we have seen, the Russians, Daesh, and the Chinese actively use information to advance their foreign policy interests. They change the "facts," alter perceptions, and shift blame. Exposing adversarial propaganda for what it is, and exposing the reality that propaganda seeks to gloss over requires agility, resources, and a strategy.

Tactically, we must first understand whether, how, and why adversarial propaganda efforts are successful. The "counter" will often not be through a bullhorn, but through a change in policy, restating a policy, or bringing other resources, including communications resources, to bear on the underlying problems that propagandists seek to exploit.

Propaganda succeeds most when it is uncontested and when audiences cannot turn elsewhere. The challenges posed by Russian, Daesh, Chinese, and Iranian propaganda, among others, may have common elements, but they will be specific in their targeting and impact.

The BBG can help several ways here, beyond professional journalism that exposes the reality on the ground and potentially inoculates against propaganda.

First, the BBG can undertake investigative journalism to expose realities our adversaries are trying to hide. The BBG does not have the resources to do this. During the Cold War, this was a focus of USIA and VOA and they had the capability to execute effectively in these areas. RFE/RL also was effective through their large staff dedicated to investigating abuses and corruption in Eastern Europe and in Soviet Russia.

While there are successful programs and efforts scattered across the BBG, in particular at RFE/RL, RFA and VOA, there is not the capacity for sustained, long-term corruption and investigative reporting. The BBG would welcome conversations with Congress and the Administration on how to continue to increase our investment into this important resource.

Second, the BBG's journalists are the "canary in the coal mine." That is because of their deep networks in countries of interest to U.S. foreign policy. Because they grew up in these countries, lived and worked in them, they often have a "feel" for what is happening on the ground. The BBG should take their views into account, especially when planning broadcast "surge" in response to crises.

It is critical that the BBG focus both its credibility and its tools to proactively counter misinformation in key audiences around the world. I look forward to working with this Committee, and the rest of the Congress, to ensure that we are coordinated in our efforts, and I would be happy to answer any additional questions you may have at any time.

Mr. WILSON. In 2011, the Administration established the Center for Strategic Counterterrorism Communications (CSCC). Its charter is to "reinforce, integrate, and complement public communications efforts across the executive branch." DOD currently has approximately six detailees assigned to the CSCC. a) How are DOD strategic, operational, and tactical plans and operations coordinated with the CSCC? b) Is the CSCC an effective organization to then integrate those plans and operations within the interagency? c) Is the CSCC appropriately resourced by DOD and other interagency partners?

Secretary LUMPKIN. Aspects of DOD plans and operations that are relevant to counterterrorism communications are closely coordinated with the CSCC. The CSCC's role is to integrate counterterrorism messaging of various U.S. Government departments and agencies. DOD detailees to the CSCC provide military expertise, including in planning which allows CSCC to be more effective in integrating DOD capabilities into U.S. Government counterterrorism messaging. DOD's support to CSCC is at the level requested and is adequate for the tasks assigned.

Mr. WILSON. Actions are a fundamental form of communication, and strategic communications can affect actions. It is therefore imperative that we make effective, credible, and timely communications a part of our operations and planning across all levels—strategic, operational, and tactical. Poorly integrated actions and messaging could degrade the mission, while simultaneously bolstering our adversary's own propaganda. a) How, where, when, and at what levels does DOD incorporate strategic communications into military planning? b) How are those plans integrated with interagency partners at the COCOM and Joint Staff level? c) How are they integrated with coalition partners? d) Are we prepared to counter state and hybrid actors, as we do non-state actors? e) How are lessons learned shared within the Joint Staff, COCOMs, and interagency partners?

Secretary LUMPKIN and General MOORE. DOD incorporates strategic communications throughout all phases of operations, from strategic to tactical levels. While acknowledging that Department of State has the lead for strategic communication outside designated areas of hostility, DOD plans for actions and activities that support USG strategic communication objectives. For example, military exercises in Eastern Europe are tangible actions that reinforce U.S. pledges of support to our partners in the region. All of our plans are shared with interagency partners for review and comment by the Office of the Secretary of Defense. Additionally, the combatant command staffs have representatives from various interagency partners on the staff. These partners are vital to providing input and perspective of their parent agency. Additionally, they are able to keep their agencies informed regarding the direction of combatant command planning efforts. Our closest coalition partners often have representatives on the Joint Staff and at the COCOMs. Provided they possess the appropriate clearances, coalition partners are full participants in our planning processes. Absent those clearances, they are integrated to the fullest extent possible while protecting USG interests. Yes, although our adversaries and potential adversaries are taking advantage of new technologies, we are prepared to counter state, non-state, and hybrid actors alike. Our experiences over the last decade have shown us that we must become more adept at dealing with all actors in the information environment and has led us to develop capabilities and authorities tailored to meet that challenge. With the advent of new technologies, our adversaries will continue to evolve their efforts against us and we must continue to rapidly adapt our capabilities and responses to address all adversaries. All IO can be submitted into the Joint Lessons Learned Process (JLLP) overseen by the J7. Joint Lessons Learned Information System (JLLIS) is the automated solution supporting implementation of the Chairman's Joint Lessons Learned Program (JLLP). JLLIS facilitates the collection, tracking, management, sharing, collaborative resolution and dissemination of lessons learned to improve the development/readiness of the Joint Force. The validated information also enables actionable Doctrine, Organization, Training, Materiel, Leadership and Education, Personnel, and Facilities (DOTMLPF) and Policy changes to improve joint and combined capabilities. The outputs JLLP include changes to Joint Doctrine, Education, Concept Development, Joint Exercises and

Joint Capabilities. All COCOM's, Functional Commands, Combat Support Agencies and Services participate. JLLP supports the interagency, multinational and non-governmental communities to foster mutual understanding and enhanced inter-operability.

Mr. WILSON. What lessons related to MISO and IO have we learned from the past 14 years of war? How do you think that will affect how the MISO/IO force of the future will need to change in the next 5 to 10 years?

General HAAS. Based upon our experiences and lessons learned over the last 14 years, we have adjusted our personnel selection, updated and enhanced our MISO training, and better integrated our force structure. We have implemented a new personnel assessment and selection program, which lasts two weeks, and is designed to test potential members of the MISO community to ensure they have the attributes necessary to conduct effective influence. We have expanded our MISO training with an increased focus on language, culture, and influence principles. Our MISO force structure now includes two active duty groups, which are combined with Special Forces and Civil Affairs Groups under one single command headquarters. This integration of capabilities allows for better fusion of all Army Special Operation Forces (ARSOF) skill sets in execution.

With respect to the future, we have seen our adversaries, both nation-state and terrorist, increasingly turn to extensive use of misinformation and propaganda as their primary efforts. These efforts have frequently taken advantage of the open nature of the Internet with alarming results. We will need to master web-based operations and stay abreast of emerging advances in technology to meet this challenge. We have learned that we must remain committed to our Special Operations Forces truths and continue to invest in our people. We must remain focused on our long term objectives, rather than being reactive and trying to match each of the adversaries' tweets/posts, etc. Our force needs to remain flexible in posture rather than settle into one operational paradigm (e.g. only deploying MISTs). We must be able to execute in a range of missions across the operational and tactical levels in evolving and ever-changing scenarios.

Mr. WILSON. What lessons related to MISO and IO have we learned from the past 14 years of war? How do you think that will affect how the MISO/IO force of the future will need to change in the next 5 to 10 years?

General MOORE. The operational environment today contains a complex mixture of audiences, media platforms and communicators all with a great appetite for information. The last 14 years have provided with a greater understanding of the cultural aspects of a specific operational environment which factors local history, religion, culture, customs, and laws. This increased understanding allows us to better understand audiences, which is essential to effectively communicate to the right audience to achieve an effect in support of our government objectives. Another lesson learned is our increased U.S. interagency collaboration at the operational, tactical, and, embassy levels, which has expanded our whole of government efforts to synchronize messages with actions. However, with increased coordination comes a slower approval processes and one must maintain a balance to ensure actions and words send the intended message.

Without a doubt, we'll continue to garner more lessons learned as the information environment evolves. In the coming years, we'll need to be more agile and flexible as our adversaries will also continue to do so, especially in the information space.